DARK NLP

How Reading Body Language to Influence Human Behavior Through Secret Mind Control Techniques of Manipulation and Persuasion and Improve Emotional Intelligence to Convince and Manage People

Robert Covert

TABLE OF CONTENTS

INTRODUCTION

What is Neuro-Linguistics Programming?

NLP is an acronym for Neuro-Linguistic Programs. Neuro is a branch of medicine that deals with nerves and the neural system; Linguistic is another name for languages, and the program is about the configuration and setting of something to work in a certain way. Therefore, in layman's terminologies, NLP is about configuring the nerves (brain communication tools) using a particular language. With NLP, you can upgrade your mindset. You can make your memory better; have better communication skills, your intelligence quotient will most likely rank higher the next time you take the test among other skills that you can improve, modify and enhance either on yourself or on someone else.

The most basic example of Neuro-Linguistic Programming is when I say to you, "do not think of a dog!" tell me what the first thing that came to your mind is? A dog, right? This is because in the short sentence lay a command "think of a dog" your unconscious mind already conjures up the image of a dog the moment the command registered before your conscious mind takes over and instructs you to not think about it. How would this help you in communicating? Let's apply this basic example in a different setup. Assume you are out in a barbecue and you have a five-year-old son who is walking dangerously close to the grill risking getting burnt by touching it. From the above example if we tell him "do not touch the grill," the command touch the grill is already given, and his brain will take a second longer to process the warning. Therefore, the best warning to give him is "go get me a skillet from mommy" the command goes in the sentence will be processed fast, and the crisis will be averted. This is just a very basic example of Neurolinguistics programming.

CHAPTER 1: NEURO-LINGUISTIC PROGRAMMING TECHNIQUES

Each of these techniques can either be used on its own or combined with others to create faster and better methods of influencing other people

ANCHORING

This NLP technique uses a touch, gesture, or word as an "anchor" for desired emotion. It is used to induce a certain emotion such as happiness or a frame of mind such as relaxation by using the "anchor" as a bookmark for the desired emotion or mood that can be used to recall it. This is better understood in an example, recall the time you were ecstatic about something, say when you had some really good news, when you had your first kiss, when you performed well in a test or when your boss congratulated you for a job well done, it can be any special moment that had you feeling out of this world, happy and elated. Now tell me about that day, give me the details of how it started and what happened before the special moment that was a happy one for you. Give me details so that I can have a vivid image of the activities, I want to be able to feel as though I was there with you too on that day, recall the moment and the feelings. As you do this, hold your left index and middle fingers in your right hand, gently give these fingers two quick squeezes. As you squeeze the second time, enlarge the picture of the happy moment and imagine the happy feeling is multiplying in strength and getting stronger. Tell the story again, think of what you are feeling current and how you felt than when you were happy, again squeeze your fingers twice and double the feeling as you enlarge the picture of the happy moment. Repeat this five times while doing the squeeze as the feeling intensifies. This is how the anchor is laid and the first step of anchoring. Later on, we can use the anchor to recall the feeling of happiness by using the gesture of squeezing the fingers twice.

Your subconscious mind associates the sign of two squeezes on your left fingers with happy therefore the more clarity you have in the feeling is shown in the number of times you lay the anchor as shown in the example above. For this technique to work effectively, the feeling has to be clear and vivid. Using this activity is known as conditioning the mind. It does not only work on human beings as shown in the experiment by Russian scientist Ivan Pavlov who rang a bell every time he fed his dogs. The resulting effect was the dogs salivated every time that the bell was rung since they had already likened the sound of a ringing bell with the filling of their stomach and the taste of food. This is the process whereby the mind controller creates an anchor in the target, so that makes it easy to put the victim in a certain state just by tapping or touching and sublimely programming the mind. Subliminal are hidden suggestions, that are only seen (heard) and processed only by your subconscious mind. They can be audio suggestions, that are in music or voice recordings or visual suggestions that are cleverly embedded into either a painting, a photograph or a design of a place whether exterior or interior. The best example I can come up with of subliminal suggest was in the movie "focus" by Will Smith who was a con man and a risk-taker. During one football game, he went to the billionaires' arena and got into a game with one of the billionaires, he asked the billionaire to pick a number of the jersey any jersey whether it is a player who was on the field, on the bench or a fan seated and cheering from the stands. The most shocking thing is the billionaire picked the same number that Will Smith had in mind. Later on, in the movie, he explained that he was able to do this by programming the billionaire's mind all day. The billionaire, who was of Asian origin had been listening to music in the elevator of his hotel room that was in mandarin and translated to the number 55 in English. I am sure most of us do not pay close attention to the music in elevators when we got in just like the billionaire. On his drive from the hotel to wherever he was going, there were some protestors there who wore the jersey that had the number fifty-five and some of them even had placards with the number written on them. At the traffic light, the billionaire saw a friend to Will smith who is the same guy who was at the field next to the players wearing a jersey number fifty-five which is the reason the billionaire picked the number. In case you missed it, it is because among the sea of strangers he saw something familiar and his subconscious mind endorsed it.

EXAMPLES OF WHEN TO USE NEURO-LINGUISTIC PROGRAMMING ANCHORING

There are different moments when NLP anchoring can be used; the most common is in rewarding someone. Take the case of a grade two mathematics teacher who pats his or her students on their backs whenever they pass, and for those who don't pass, they don't get a pat as a reward. The students will strive to pass their exams so that they get a reward. By using the pat on their back the students have attributed the pat on the back with doing well or the sense of having it under control, therefore before a test the teacher can use this pat on the back to remind them that they have everything under control and they would do well, effectively calming nerves and jitters before a test.

Similarly, a martial arts coach can use anchoring to improve his student's feeling of reward whenever they do well, for instance, after sparring. Traditionally after a spar, the fighters will shake their hands; a coach who feels his student has put up a good fight can give a light punch on their arm to show this. Sparring is an intense session that is accompanied by adrenaline and endorphins (pleasurable feeling) when the coach uses the light punch on the arm as an anchor after the handshake, and the students will associate the post adrenaline endorphins with the reward. Later on, before a fight or before grading by judges, the coach can use this anchor (the light punch) to help their students calm their nerves by giving them a light punch on the shoulder.

Neuro-Linguistic Programming anchoring can also be employed in seduction as will be explained in detail late on in this book. In the meantime, though try doing an exercise of applying to anchor on either yourself or someone you work with, spouse or kids. Remember it may take a while before you see the results; therefore, Good luck remembers practice makes perfect.

SWISH

The swish pattern is a Neuro-Linguistic Programming technique that is used in replacing an unfavorable behavior or emotion with a more useful one. It is a copy and paste system where you copy the emotion associated with doing one thing and pasting over the emotion elicited by another. It can be used to make the "bad" activities such as going to the gym, eating salad seem better by applying a different emotion such as the happy emotion elicited when eating a chocolate cake. The idea of the swish technique is to keep on switching back and forth between two images with one feeling in mind.

Imagine you have changed your jobs and tomorrow you start work at a new company, the idea of going to a new environment is scary, you will feel anxious about meeting a new boss, how will you fit in with your colleagues will they like you, will you like them. Is it the wrong decision for you to change jobs? These questions will elicit feelings of worry, anxiety, and nervousness, among others. The odds of you projecting these feelings to the new employees is very high if this is what you will be feeling, therefore you must swap the feeling of anxiety whenever you think of the first day at work with a more comfortable feeling like excitement. How do you do this?

First, think of a memory that got you excited like going to the fun park when you were younger, or attending a party with your friends, think about the emotion, the excitement of adventure you will have while thinking about this quickly switch to the thought of your first day at work tomorrow and right before the feeling of anxiety creeps in switch back to the idea of going out with friends. Do this a couple of times holding onto the feeling of excitement as you "swish" back and forth between the two mental pictures. As this is happening the conscious memory is trying to blind the subconscious memory into associating the good feeling with both events to overcome the bad memory.

APPLICATION OF THE SWISH TECHNIQUE

Very few of us like exercising, no one like the pain and the aches that come with hitting the gym every single time. The idea of the soreness and how tired we will be after the exercises; it is no wonder people have gym memberships that they rarely utilize fully. How about a little exercise, before you groan I mean a mental exercise, think about going to a camp with your family or friends. The adventure, the thrill of sleeping out by the fire, the joy of exchanging stories around the bonfire, the amazing nights of roasting meat and marshmallows under the stars. Now think about going to the gym, think about the different people you will meet there, think about the campfire the different people who you just met seated around the campfire, think about the gym and the different equipment there, think about the camp and the different equipment and supplies you will need for camping, do this several times switch back and forth between the two mental pictures without letting the positive feeling disappear. After about ten times of this swishing, you will be feeling pretty excited about going to the gym and ready for the adventure. If it doesn't work, do it again with a different thought that you are particularly excited about. Remember, you need to do a lot of practice to master this technique.

PATTERN INTERRUPTION

This is a technique where the listeners' inner monologue (voice in the head) or subconscious train of thought is tapped into and lured into either a sequence or a pattern. When this pattern has already been established, the listener is the roughly pulled from it right before a very critical part of the pattern completion. This will leave them wondering what is going to happen in their subconscious mind, and their conscious mind will be distracted by this abrupt change in the system. Derren Brown talked to strangers, and using this technique, he had them giving him their wallets in twenty seconds.

LOOP BREAK

This is the use of a technique that will break the looping process of your body that gets you into states of anxiety, fear, stress, rage, and anger. This involves manipulating the conscious mind to stop the unconscious mind from carrying out an activity that it assumes is natural. This technique is employed to help one control their own

Behavior. Its simplicity makes it very easy for one also to introduce a loop break in someone else's thoughts to control their behaviors too. The deep emotions, such as anger need to be triggered by something or someone for them to manifest. For instance, if you are in stuck in traffic and running late to work but a driver hits your rear end on the highway, the most logic thing for you to do is to let them go after you have picked their insurance information, but more often than not you will get out of your car angry and waste more time arguing or even get into a fight with the said person. While you may end up feeling good about giving the driver a piece of your mind, it is not the productive action you would have taken, but the anger that you are feeling will impair your judgment and ruin our cognitive ability leading to more time-wasting and efforts. The reason we get more agitated quickly is because of a loop that runs between our memory, our body and the amygdala (the region in our brain responsible for emotion) while bypassing the region of the brain that is responsible for moderating our behaviors known as the frontal lobe.

CHAPTER 2: WHY IS NLP SO NOTORIOUSLY CONTROVERSIAL?

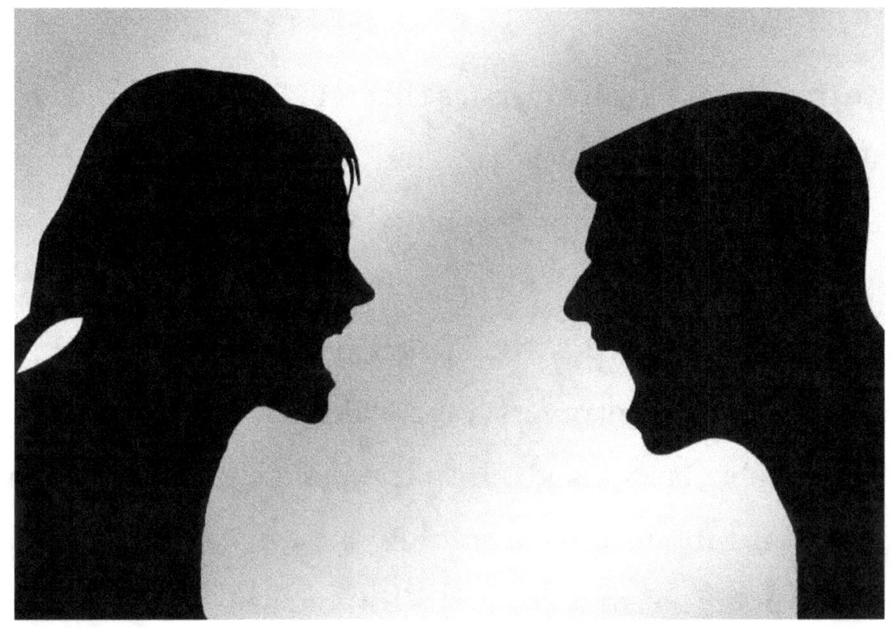

You will now receive full access into the world of Dark NLP. It is important to remember that the principles and techniques of this school of thought are in direct contradiction to mainstream morality and social norms, so you should be prepared to have your preconceptions challenged. This chapter will begin with several real-life examples of how the power of NLP can change lives for better or for worse. We will then explore some of the darkest and most controversial uses of NLP that have ever been devised. The chapter will conclude with a look at the range of controversies centering around NLP that have taken place over the years.

By exploring the controversies that NLP has generated, you will gain a range of insights. First, you will see that often NLP is criticized not for the actual content it contains but for its ability to challenge widely held viewpoints. Anything that goes against the grain of popular thought is bound to court controversy, regardless of what it teaches. You will also gain insight into the power of NLP to grant additional influence to absolutely anyone. Anything that has the potential to disrupt the established social order is seen as controversial and NLP is no exception.

THE POWER OF NLP - REAL LIFE EXAMPLES

Next, we will look at a range of insights into the power that NLP has to influence lives. This section does not seek to take a moral stance on the NLP examples that are provided, rather seeks only to use them to show the immense power of NLP when used effectively. The ideas from each story will be extracted and explained so that you understand exactly what has taken place in each of the examples and why the results have occurred.

One powerful example of NLP is how it can cure people of addictions that negatively impact their life. One such story is of a man who visited an NLP therapist complaining of his inability to give up smoking cigarettes. Even though he had experienced bad health effects as a result of his habit and was spending a lot of money on three packs a day, he had been unable to find the motivation to give up.

The NLP therapist was able to use a series of envisioning techniques to replace the view that the man had of cigarettes. Instead of seeing them as a guilty pleasure, the man swapped his imagery of cigarettes with that of death and bad health. As a result of manipulating his internal viewpoint, the man no longer desired cigarettes and was able to quit.

Another testament to the power of NLP stems from the world of business. One high-ranking female executive in a European division of a technology company was summoned to a meeting in America with an intimidating executive. Although she was well respected within her division of the company, she had achieved this by being likable and genuinely supportive of those she worked with. She did not have a high level of assertion and was therefore fearful of the meeting in America.

The woman decided to visit an NLP teacher to learn some ways by which she could feel more comfortable and confident about the meeting in America. She was taught an NLP technique known as anchoring in which she was able to link emotion to a physical trigger. In this case, she was taught to think back through her past to a time when she felt confident and in control of what was taking place. She was able to do this. She was then instructed to link this feeling to a ball of colored light. She was then told to move this colored light onto the floor in front of her and use it to draw a circle around her. This gave the woman an immense feeling of total security and confidence within the boundaries of the circle.

When it came time for the woman's meeting in America, she was able to draw upon this technique and use it to get rid of her fears about interacting with the executive. She was able to calmly and collectedly deal with the situation at hand. It turns out she was not even being criticized or disciplined and they merely wanted to discuss strategy with her. Because of her NLP training, however, she was able to avoid experiencing the negative impact of stress and worry.

Some of the most controversial but effective users of NLP have used it in their pursuit of romance. For now, a brief insight will be provided into how effective this can be.

One of the most well-known teachers of NLP runs seminars in which men learn how to use NLP based methods to induce good feelings in members of the opposite sex and increase their chances of having a successful romantic encounter. The methods revolve around somewhat esoteric ideas such as generating a positive internal state which can then be passed on to the other person through the law of state transference.

The examples provided so far are some of the more positive and acceptable uses of NLP in people's lives. It should be noted that ideas such as these exist on the fringe of the NLP community - they are not widely accepted or even known about. They are the dark secrets of the NLP world which are about to be widely revealed for the very first time.

THE DARKEST REAL WORLD NLP EXAMPLES

One dark area of application for NLP has been within the schools of seduction based around this area Of influence. While the majority of men and women using the ideas behind NLP to help their chances of success in the dating world do so in a mainstream and acceptable way, a few fringe figures have devoted themselves to learning darkly devastating applications for NLP teachings. You are advised to read on with caution as the following ideas are deadly if in the wrong hands.

Patterns are a common way of referring to the dark NLP techniques that are used for seduction purposes. A series of patterns gained notoriety within the seduction community and became to be known as the banned patterns. They earned this name due to the fact they were deemed far too dark and amoral for the community to accept. Due to their notoriety, they have often been sought out by the community, but are hard to find. They are presented here in full.

One such pattern is known as 'the shadow and the rising sun.' It is widely banned within the seduction community due to the fact that it draws upon the ideas found in Jungian psychology to unlock a woman's dark side, the hidden shadow of her personality.

This is achieved by the seducer beginning to talk about the idea of contrasts. He focused on talking about contrasting imagery that can evoke the idea of darkness such as light and dark, day and night and yin and yang. He talks about how a dark side is an essential part of life and without one, nothing is meaningful. He then begins to talk about how everyone has a dark side. This can be seen as the idea of a rising sun which casts a shadow and changes the perspective on everything. The seducer then invites the target to step into her dark side and view the world through its lens. This is intended to put the target into a susceptible state where they behave in a way that they otherwise would not.

Another technique that is often used in conjunction with the above technique is known as the hospital pattern. In this pattern, the seducer fluctuates his target's emotional state between extreme feelings of pleasure and extreme feelings of pain. This rapid change of emotional states, which swing back and forth multiple times, is intended to leave the target feeling emotionally unstable and therefore susceptible to influence. When the target is in this susceptible state, the seducer can anchor the target's perception of pleasure to himself, and the perception of pain to something other than himself. By doing this, the seducer can ensure that the target feels immense pleasure associated with the seducer, who can trigger these feelings on demand.

Another dark usage of NLP in the pursuit of seduction is something known as a pattern interrupt. This is where the seducer uses Dark NLP to stop his target from doing something he does not want and to reduce her rationality and defense mechanisms. For example, if the target begins to list logical reasons why she should not be with the seducer, the seducer may ask her something unrelated like "What's your favorite color?" By doing this, the seducer disrupts the target's thought process and therefore defense mechanisms. This stops the target from falling into their habitual patterns.

NLP has also been used in a dark way to make people question which of their memories are real and which are fabricated. There is a technique in which the target is put into a state of relaxation that is often likened to being somewhere between awake and asleep. In this state, the target is deeply suggestible. The target is guided back through their memories until the user of Dark NLP finds a memory they wish to disrupt. They then ask a series of questions that are intended to make the target doubt if the memory ever actually occurred or if they imagined it. This can be used to disrupt the target's feeling of identity and make them question the beliefs and values they have about who they are. This is often the first step in the process of brainwashing someone into having a new identity.

A similar technique can be used to implant false memories into a target's mind which is perceived as real. Just as in the last technique, the target is put into a state of deep relaxation, in which they become susceptible to influence. They are then led back through their memories. At the appropriate point, the target is asked a series of leading questions into remembering something that didn't happen. This often begins with a real memory, and then the target will be asked things such as "Then do you remember when x happened?" and "'How did you feel when x happened?" By latterly framing the question, the target's brain focuses on recalling an emotional response. Since the fact the event has taken place is presented as a statement, the brain assumed it to be true. This is used to make people remember things that have never happened to them, such as when cults cause victims to imagine they have suffered abuse from their parents that never actually took place. This is often used to separate a target from their environment.

THE CONTROVERSY OF NLP

NLP has proven to be one of the most controversial subsets of psychology. We will now explore a range of the controversies that NLP has generated and explore exactly why this discipline is perceived as so troubling and controversial by the mainstream. In doing this, the power of NLP will be clearly illustrated and shown in a way that highlights how far outside the boundaries of mainstream thought NLP, and in particular, Dark NLP really is.

Some of the earliest criticisms of NLP came from within the mainstream psychology profession. Traditional therapists and psychologists stated that NLP was dangerous as it took shortcuts to achieve results that were only possible after prolonged, traditional therapy. The psychologists stated that taking these shortcuts meant that people were not truly healed; rather they just learned to bury their traumas even deeper. The NLP world hit back and stated that the psychology profession was just worried as their slow results were becoming less and less acceptable to people. The fight for legitimacy is something that has coexisted with NLP since its initial days.

One controversy surrounding NLP is the fact that it is seen as encouraging immoral behavior. Because NLP teaches people how to deeply understand and influence others, it is seen as encouraging people to act in ways that will be detrimental and selfish. NLP teachers have hit back and said it is unfair to single out NLP for this criticism. Almost any school of thought can be used for good or for bad, and it is not the fault of anyone but the individual using techniques for immoral purposes.

Many people, particularly within feminist circles, have criticized the use of NLP for seduction. They state that it removes the element of choice and makes people do things they would not normally agree to. The counter-argument to this perspective is that NLP can be used to genuinely enhance a romantic encounter and help people feel a greater range of positive emotions. The majority of people using NLP for romantic purposes do so with good intentions. The few individuals who do not are to blame for any blameworthy uses, not the ideas themselves.

The model of teaching NLP has also been criticized over the years. It has been alleged that the environment in which NLP is taught is similar to a cult as people are encouraged to accept the NLP principles without question and are not to engage in critical thought. Opposers claim that NLP certifications are administered without careful enough training or testing being carried out. NLP teaching schools have hit back against this criticism and instead insisted that people are free to believe or not believe what they are taught and that NLP teachers have no means of suppressing free thought. They also insist that people only receive NLO certification after they are ready to, and criticisms in this area stem from the traditional therapy industry worrying about the disruptive potential of NLP.

CHAPTER 3: MIND CONTROL AND NLP FOR RELATIONSHIPS

We all want to create relationships with ease. No one wants to feel lonely or unable to fit in with others. According to researches, success is mostly based on the relationships one creates. People who can initiate and maintain good, mutual and productive relationships with others are more likely to succeed compared to those who do not maintain rapport.

Building good relationships do not come naturally to everyone. However, with NLP tools and perspectives, this skill can be learned and developed.

In any relationship, communication is inevitable. Basically, communication does not stop. Even when a couple fights and the two people give each other silent treatment, communication is still going on - they are telling each other about the stress, anger, and manipulation quietly.

If a frustrated teenager chooses to eat dinner in his/her room behind closed doors, He/she is communicating something to himself and the family. Even in the most neural situations, people still communicate through body language and movement of the eyes.

Simply, understanding that communication is continuously taking place can make a huge difference in most relationships. Since much of our communication is indirect, unconscious and nonverbal, knowing the messages we pass through body language and eye contact can help us to become more conscious of the things, we say and do to others. Human beings send out signals to each other all the time and becoming more aware of how we pass the message is the first step to better relationships.

In the book titled awareness, the writer, Antony de Mello states that awareness can help us to change our lives a great deal. If one was to do nothing else apart from becoming more conscious off his/her habits, it would make a great difference in relationships. In fact, good communication can help you to get things done. Good communication helps a person to build confidence and consequently to ward off manipulators.

Communication involves understanding that the perceptions of other people are not necessarily wrong if they differ from ours. We tend to think that the way we see things is right and the only reality. NLP reminds us that our opinion of the word is developed through the filters we have developed for ourselves over the years, such as values and expectations.

Once we acknowledge that our perception is not the only reality, then it becomes easier to understand and communicate with others. We cannot see the world in the same way because everyone has a different model and map, leading to different behaviors. Such an understanding can help you to deal with different people, including the manipulators.

 The first habit of highly successful people is to understand then seek to be understood. In today's world, most of us are in a rush; therefore, we have no time to understand others before responding. Many of us listen to reply rather than to receive the message. NLP informs us that our map of the world is not a territory that requires protection. We can benefit more from understanding the maps of other people rather than staying in our own cocoons.

The people with good communication skills, high levels of understanding, and flexible behavior are more likely to control situations compared to the rigid ones. Even in the wild, animals, and plants that adapt to the changes in the environment very fast are more likely to survive longer than others. Businesses that accommodate the changes in the economy and social environments are more successful than those opposing them. The same applies to individuals.

A person who understands the maps believes and practices of others can switch between them and reach a wider variety of people. He/she will also be able to establish good and lasting relationships. Anyone who becomes rigid to one way of doing things and thinking will gradually be left become irrelevant as the world changes.

Strong relationships are formed on communication. Without communication, people will not know how to handle others. For instance, if a person is doing something which you do not like and you fail to tell him/her so, he/she will probably do the same things without realizing they are affecting you. However, if you respectfully express yourself, the person will avoid hurting you. A manipulator needs to be addressed firmly and effectively to deter him/her.

The true meaning of communication is found in the response it produces and the results we get. In most cases, we blame others for failing to understand us. However, NLP teaches us that we are responsible for passing the message, and if the other person does not understand, we need to change our method of communication. Again, all this is about flexibility – being able to understand others and adopting their ways. To pass the message across, you sometimes have to communicate in terms of the other person, by first understanding his/her world, and getting to know the map. You need to put your perspective aside for a while and assess things from the other side.

In life, people do the best they can with what they have. For instance, when a child falls down, he/she begins to scream or cry. Why? Because he/she knows that crying and screaming will attract the attention of an adult who will help. Experience has taught the child. Adults tend to use more complex and sophisticated ways, but the same principle from childhood holds – we do what will give the best results.

According to NLP, every behavior has a positive intention even though we might not understand. Developing and maintaining relationships is basically about understanding why people behave the way they do – not from our perspective but theirs. Good relationships are also about helping each other to identify and adopt more productive behaviors and giving each other the required resources. Truthfully, the majority of us are doing the best we can with what we have. Consequently, the best gift to offer someone is a new tool. You might not be able to solve someone's challenges, but giving them the chance to do so will help to strengthen your relationship.

NLP encourages us to take responsibility and helps us to understand that people operate from one of the two perspectives – cause and effect. When a person is operating 'at cause,' he/she sees that the control is in his/her hand and that it is possible to change or improve the situation. On the other hand, a person operating 'at effect,' blames other people for the current circumstances. When 'at effect,' we blame others for our failures. When ta effect, we take the responsibility and strive to improve the situation.

In all the perspectives, the truth is that we are in control of our circumstances – deciding where we should work. If a relationship is not working out the way you hoped, there are high chances of blaming the other person. A majority of us will want the other person to be put to task for our failures. The ideal plan should be to assess your own behavior and identify things that need to be changed within you. When operating 'at cause,' you are more likely to improve your circumstances than when at effect. NLP will help you to act from at cause through seeking to understand the perspective of the other person and listening to them to help.

NLP helps us to build better relationships by making us understand that people are not their behavior. Technically, all of us are doing the best we can with what we have. The resources we have at our disposal are major determinants of our behaviors. If we had more or fewer resources and a different perspective, we would behave differently. Such an understanding can help you build a better relationship and deal with manipulators.

Do not label people based on their current behavior, may be given a different circumstance, and they would act better or worse. Maybe that manipulator had a very rough childhood, thus making him/her feel the need to be tougher than everyone else. Maybe the mind controller is feeling weak and afraid on the inside and is looking for ways to act have control. Note, however, that you do not have to allow people to manipulate you just because you are feeling empathic. Even though that empathy is pushing you to help such people, do not make yourself a victim – Protect yourself first. After all, you cannot offer what you do not have.

Behaviors change all the time as we grow and learn. What we consider as bad relationships can be turned around using NLP, once we learn how to be proactive and take control.

CHAPTER 4: NLP AND YOU

Neuro-Linguistic Programming is used today for a variety of different things. It can be helpful in helping people overcome issues like anxiety, PTSD, and fears. These are only a very few issues that Neuron-Linguistic Programming can help with. While some people use it for good, others use it for darker desires.

We would love to say that the only place you will find NLP is in your therapist's office, however, we see it in everyday life. From your workplace to the ads on your social media accounts, you can see it everywhere. NLP does not only focus on what people say but more importantly focus on what people are doing. Our body language says more than our mouths ever could.

NLP has been under the debate of whether it is an actual science or if it is considered a pseudoscience. The debate still exists today and it is hard to pinpoint this science due to the fact that it has not gone through the same rigorous testing as therapies such as CBT, Cognitive Behavioral Therapy.

There is a pretty broad range of techniques used within NLP and this also makes it difficult to lock down which pieces work. There have been some studies performed and oftentimes the results were inconclusive. In some, it appears as if NLP had made a true improvement in subjects with psychosis, instability, and other unwanted traits. Others worked on looking at its effectiveness to help issues like PTSD and anxiety. The results came back exceptionally varied.

Neuro-Linguistic Programming has been around for more than forty years. For something to be around this long and continue to be used throughout many people's daily lives means there has got to be some validity to it, right? We see it used so widely on a commercial level and it certainly does have an impact.

It also has its place in the world of Psychology and Dark Psychology. Due to the fact that it is quite unstructured, it is difficult to show true proof of its success. There are also a plethora of different ideas and ways of executing NLP. For some, it is a very effective form of therapy that truly helps them lead better lives. For others, it may not benefit them at all. These people will need to look at more traditional therapies to work through their issues and lead a happier and mentally healthier life.

NLP HISTORY

NLP is, in a way, a method of mind control. It was developed by a team of people. However, the majority of the credit is given to, two California boys, John Grinder, and Richard Bandler. In the 1970s, they decided to combine the works of Virginia Satir, a therapist for families, Freidrich Perls, a psychotherapist, and a hypnotherapist by the name of Milton Erickson. They wanted to take the heart of linguistic therapy and improve it. Find the pieces that truly worked and make something better.

The three people that they studied were chosen due to the fact that they had better results with their clients than most others in their field. People found their success to be odd and uncommon. Naturally, inquisitive minds wanted to know what these people had in common and why their methods worked so well. They studied them in live sessions and via videotape.

NLP is subtle. When we think about normal hypnotherapy, we think about people falling asleep and acting out strange and silly acts. Realistically, it is used for much more meaningful purposes. For example, people use hypnotherapy to help them stop smoking or to deal with traumas of the past that may have not been coped with.

NLP does things a bit differently. It is much more suggestive and not so in your face.

In the beginning, Neuro-Linguistic Programming was thought to be as helpful as products like "snake juice" from the days of the old west. However, as the seventies turned into the eighties it became more and more accepted. Businesses were jumping on the bandwagon to learn about it so they could, in turn, use it to help them gain profits from consumers. Also, everyone from therapists to political figures started to want the information on this type of "programming". It seriously started to blow up in terms of popularity.

Companies became interested in NLP because it can help them communicate more clearly. This helps to improve the performance of employees and the overall performance of the business. Businesses that use NLP have experienced better growth in their companies as a whole.

Not only can it help people become better negotiators it can also help them stay motivated. When you feel comfortable at work and you feel like everyone is giving it their all, it's easy to build a solid team. Being a confident leader that pays attention to tone, body language, and verbiage will help lead to better success. Implementing the practices of NLP can promote growth for companies.

As people started to employ these tactics, they started to notice changes in their teams. Boosts in morale and productivity. Now we see NLP happening around us every day. This is not necessarily a bad thing as people that practice NLP tend to be more self-aware. In turn, they tend to make better choices that are made from rationality rather than emotions.

There are four main points to NLP, they are referred to as the Pillars of NLP. They are Behavioral Flexibility, Rapport, Outcome Thinking, and Sensory Awareness. Each one is of equal importance as the others. Taking the time to look briefly at each one of these points gives a better understanding of NPL as a whole and how it can help you weed out the fakers in your life.

The first pillar we are going to look at is Behavioral Flexibility. This means to go with the flow. When people can see that the tactic they are currently using isn't working and adapt their behavior it can have great results. Being able to quickly change your perspective will allow more people to understand you.

The next aspect we are going to look at is Rapport. Creating a good rapport with someone is simply getting them to trust you quickly. Besides, it is the ability to form quick relationships with people. It is easy to build rapport by using a common language, being polite, and showing empathy. There are many ways to build a good rapport with a person, these are only a few.

Then we move on to Outcome Thinking. It is exactly what it states, spending the time to think about the end result of what you want. Oftentimes, people get stuck on a certain point, that is commonly negative. It consumes the thought pattern and can make choosing the correct route to where you want to go difficult. With outcome thinking you are always working toward an end goal. This can promote better decision making along the way.

Lastly, we have Sensory Awareness. Being aware of your surroundings plays a major role in knowing what is going on. When you walk into a public place and you take notice of the tone of the room, the colors surrounding you, the groups of people, it can be very enlightening. It can also help you easily understand how you need to behave in that situation.

The more you learn about these four pillars the more success you will have with NLP. They are the foundation and anyone who wants to learn NLP will spend a lot of time on each one. The more you broaden your knowledge the more you will be able to apply what you have learned to your daily life and the more protected you will be from the ones that want to manipulate you, control you, or cause other burdens in your life.

NLP has grown and changed over the years. What started out as focusing on what people's eyes were doing, the words they choose to use, and building quick rapport, turned into something much, much more. All sciences grow and change over time and we imagine that this one will also continue to evolve.

After focusing on what the yes were doing, word choice, and rapport this therapy started to grow and focus on other aspects. In the '80s, the people using NLP were focusing on what it is that causes feelings inside of us. This helped therapists to figure out how to help someone deal with their individual problems.

More and more people started using the techniques found with NPL but they wanted to put different names to it. To say they had come up with it all on their own. When it comes down to it, no matter what you call it, NPL is the same across the globe. Today, it is used not only to help you have control and choices in how you react, but it can also help you figure out what other people are up to.

The people in the here and now that are using NPL have a variety of different reasons for doing it. Some of it is to help themselves become better people while for others it is about weeding out the rats in their lives. Businesses use it in team-building and marketing techniques. Here again, we can see how vast the world of Neuro-Linguistic Programming really is.

It has been said that people who study Neuro-Linguistic Programming live freely. They can access all different types of situations and make choices in how they choose to proceed instead of being led by instinct and emotion. How you think, feel, behave, and speak can all be choices you make that can help you lead the best life possible.

NLP can be used throughout your daily life in a huge variety of ways. Some common reasons that people start using this are that they want to motivate other people, have control over their emotions, conquer their fears, communicate more effectively, and find success in life. There are many other reasons a person would take an interest in NLP.

If you are unsure of who you can trust in your crowd NLP can seriously help. Understanding the behaviors and actions of people can help to clue you in on what's going on around you. This falls into Sensory Awareness. It is amazing what you can learn from looking at someone's body position and paying attention to things like their tone of voice. People really do tell you everything you need to know with very little conversation.

Whether you are at your job or heading for a late-night party downtown honing these skills can keep you mentally and physically protected against predators. Knowing NLP techniques can also inform you when other people are using it for darker desires. Many people use these practices to become their best selves, however, others have more nefarious intent.

Obviously, when you can adapt in a situation and make well-thought-out choices you are going to be more successful. There is less of a chance that people will be able to take advantage of you. Besides, you will be able to better understand the people in your life. Weeding out the keepers from the trash is simpler when you can read the situation accurately and adjust so that you are working toward your desired outcome.

Among the groups of the Dark Triad, there is a conglomeration of personality traits that are oftentimes, seen in criminals. It is not terribly surprising to find that most criminals have quite a bit in common. Taking notice of these dark traits is a great way of figuring out if someone has malicious intent toward you or not.

There are a variety of different dark traits that we see on an everyday basis. You may know someone who is very spiteful. Anyone that does something they don't like will pay for it. Sometimes it will be petty retaliation but it can explode into something much more dangerous, depending on who you are dealing with. Criminals tend to be spiteful, as they have malicious intent with their transgressions.

Another dark trait that you want to watch out for is egoism. When someone is so self-absorbed and focused on their achievements that they will run everyone else around them into the ground, it is a major problem. Some criminals scramble their way to the top because of their giant egos and their ability to only care about themselves. Keeping an eye on a big ego can save you a lot of trouble, especially in relationships and business.

Have you ever met someone that had loose morals? You know that person that doesn't have much regard for if what they are doing is right or wrong. Someone that even when they know what they are doing is wrong, does it anyway, and then just laughs it off. This is a personality trait referred to as moral disengagement. Obviously, the ability to commit a crime and not feel terrible about it is something common among criminals a pretty dark trait.

That person will go to any means to get what they want. They are the ones that are the masters of manipulation. The justification for what they are doing is always solid. When trying to track down criminals these are some of the hardest to catch as they tend to also be some of the smartest out there. Even experts of NLP can have a hard time locking this trait down.

Entitlement or Psychological Entitlement are also dark traits that we commonly see in criminals and everyday adversaries. Unfortunately, the world's sense of entitlement has gone off the rails. Nowadays, it is natural to meet people that have a sense of entitlement and this can make it difficult to use this trait in determining somebody's true intent.

Self-interest is another trait that you need to watch out for. We all have tendencies to be selfish, however, for some people, it is to an extreme. They simply do not care what other people feel or want. This is commonly seen by people boasting about how much money they have or their status. Also, their self-interest could be used to motivate them in gaining betterment in finances or society. Those that are self-interested also tend to be extremely manipulative.

Then we have the narcissist. They need attention and commonly and inflated sense of self. they will go to great extremes to prove that they are better than those that are around them. this could be in how they look, how they think, or how they act. The narcissist thinks that their ideas are the best and therefore criminal intent goes hand-in-hand with the narcissist.

Psychopathy means that you are lacking in the ability to empathize with people. They have an extreme lack of concern where others are involved. This dark trait can also lead to a lack of self-control and extremely impulsive behaviors. When thinking about criminals, this trait rings true for many of the extreme horrors we have witnessed in the past.

A sadist is a person that likes to inflict pain. They take pleasure in causing other people pain. This does not necessarily have to be physical pain. Many sadists find joy and completely tearing you down mentally. A wide variety of criminal classes fall into this category and it is a common trait that we see in many of the people that are committing heinous crimes.

CHAPTER 5: ADVANCED TECHNIQUES AND SUGGESTIBILITY TESTING

At this point, we have learned about various methods of manipulation through neuro-linguistic programming and hypnosis. By now you are armed with a plethora of weapons to use on any given subject, and you are prepared defensively if someone attempts to use any of these tactics against you. In this chapter, we will go over a couple of new topics that aren't manipulation tactics in and of themselves – they are nonetheless crucial for knowing upon whom to deploy these tactics on and for the defense of the manipulator.

SUGGESTIBILITY TESTING

Many hypnotists will tell you that suggestibility testing is best left to the street performers and entertainment hypnotists. This may be true as it has limited viability in hypnotherapy but what many hypnotists don't think about is everyday manipulation. Suggestibility testing is vastly utilizable in the realm of conversational hypnosis and everyday hypnosis towards the ends of manipulation. So what it is?

Suggestibility testing can refer to any number of verbal or physical "feelers" that help the hypnotist determine whether or not their subject is a good target for hypnosis and manipulation. They can serve as a guide for one to determine how likely a subject will bend to their will. Some hypnotists use suggestibility training to determine how deep into a hypnotic trance their subjects are but our purposes will be a little different.

For our intents and purposes, we will use suggestibility testing to find our subjects in the first place. The reason anyone would want to use suggestibility testing is to find the right subject for manipulation. The caveat with hypnotism, even conversational hypnosis, is that some people are more suggestible to others. In other words, some people are less likely to be inducted into hypnosis than others. For this reason, Dark NLP practitioners often use suggestibility testing to have a better idea of who they can manipulate and who they might not be able to.

The reason you will want to learn these tests is essential for efficiency. For example, you wouldn't want to use a lot of your time and effort trying to manipulate someone whom you've tested to have low suggestibility. It would just take too long and besides, there are tons of easily suggestible targets to choose from. It is estimated that as much as 80%

of the population is in the average range of hypnotic suggestibility – meaning that up to 80% of the population can be successfully hypnotized with moderate effort.

That is why suggestibility testing is so useful for the Dark NLP practitioner. It gives a good guideline on who a prime subject might be and helps the practitioner avoid difficult subjects.

Suggestibility tests can be deployed fairly easily. Let's take a look at some of the best methods for testing suggestibility.

The Light/Heavy Hands Technique

This method of suggestibility testing depends heavily on the concentration and that imagination of the subject. How keenly a person can bring their concentration and imagination into alignment is a very important factor. It will determine how susceptible they will be to actual hypnotic suggestion.

In this test, you will be able to see a physical manifestation of their level of suggestion. It is sometimes called the book and balloon test as well and you will see why in just a moment. The idea behind this test is to see just how deeply one can delve into their own minds. The belief is that the body will react physically if someone is concentrating on something that they believe is true. If you see that your subject reacts bodily to the light/heavy hands technique then they are more than likely a prime target for Dark NLP and hypnosis. So here is what you are going to want to do:

Ask someone, or multiple people, to close their eyes and hold their arms straight out in front of them. Tell them to have one hand turned palm-up to the sky and one hand palm-down to the ground. Now tell them to imagine that in the hand that is facing toward the sky, they are carrying a watermelon. In the hand they have facing the ground, tell them that there are a bunch of helium balloons tied to their wrist.

Go into detail about the watermelon. They can smell it, feel its rind and most importantly, feel how heavy it is. With each passing moment, their arms are getting more and more fatigued from the weight of the heavy watermelon. Meanwhile, the arm with the balloons tied to it is getting lighter as the balloons are slowly and gently ascending towards the sky. What you should be doing while their eyes are closed is seeing if their arms are moving. If they are, then you've most likely found your subject.

THE AMNESIA TECHNIQUE

The amnesia technique is a verbal test. In it, you will ask the potential subject to forget about something for some time (it shouldn't be more than a few minutes). For example, you can ask your subject to forget the letter P. Tell them to pretend that the letter P never existed and to forget that you even told them to forget about it. Then ask them to recite the alphabet. People who are moderately or highly suggestible will skip over the letter P (or whatever letter you tell them to forget) and not even realize it. Once again, if the person you tried this test on skips over the letter you told them to forget, they may be a good subject to zone in on.

THE LOCKED HAND TECHNIQUE

The locked hand technique (also known as the handclasp technique) is another physical test that the subject will have to be willing to participate in. Like the light/heavy hand technique, it will test just how deeply a person can concentrate on the words you are saying to them and what you are telling them to imagine. Ask your subject to clap their hands together and keep them together, palm to palm. Then tell them to interlace their fingers. Make sure that you maintain a fixed eye-contact with them throughout this test and tell them to push their hands together as tightly as they can. Tell them to imagine their hands merging into one piece of solid flesh and bone. After a minute or two, tell them to stop pushing and try pulling their hands apart. Again, a potential manipulation subject will find it hard to pull their hands away from each other.

CHAPTER 6: HOW TO OVERCOME MANIPULATION

Reasons we allow ourselves to be manipulated

The only time when manipulation is considered successful is the time when you allow it to control your emotions and thoughts. Thus, you must start to distinguish what is going on in you that allows you to be easily manipulated by other people. The three most basic reasons we let ourselves to be manipulated are as follows:

- **Fear**

This emotion comes in numerous structures. We, as human beings, tend to fear losing a relationship; we may fear the disapprobation of other people; we dread to make somebody discontent with our actions. We additionally dread the dangers and outcomes of the manipulator's actions. Imagine a scenario in which they prevail at doing what they threaten.

- **Guilt**

Today, we are clouded by the idea and responsibility that we should dependably prioritize the needs and wants of other people rather than our own. At times when people would talk about the right to fulfill their own needs and wants, manipulators frequently abuse us and endeavor to allow us to feel like we are accomplishing something immoral if we do not generally put their needs and wants in front of our own. Those individuals who are skilled at these manipulative tactics would tend to define love as the act of fulfilling their needs and wants as part of your obligation. Hence, if we have an opinion that goes against their beliefs, we are manipulated into thinking that we are heartless; at this point, they would make us feel very regretful of our existence and would use guilt to manipulate us.

• **Being too nice**

We appreciate being a provider, fulfilling individuals, and dealing with the needs of other people. We discover fulfillment. Moreover, our confidence would regularly originate from doing what we can for other people. In any case, at times when there is a lack of an unmistakable feeling of these and fair limitations, skilled manipulators can detect this in people who are easy targets of this phenomenon, and will use certain tactics to further their own selfish gains.

What you need to do to overcome manipulation

We have come to a point where we are here to talk about the basic skills to overcome manipulation. Moreover, manipulation would only work if you allow them to control you. Much like hypnosis, any hypnosis is actually self-hypnosis. What we are trying to state here is that knowledge that you are being manipulated defeats its entire purpose.

- **Establish a clear sense of self**

There is a need to know your identity, what your needs and wants are, what your emotions are, and what you are fond of and not fond of. You must learn to accept these and not become apologetic, as these are the things that make you. At times, we dread that in the event of speaking up, we are viewed by others as egotistical and called out for being selfish. Nevertheless, knowing your identity or what you really need in life is not at all an act of selfishness. Self-centeredness is demanding that you always get what you want or that other has always put your needs and wants first. Similarly, when another person calls you out for not following their orders or fulfilling their needs and wants, they are the ones being selfish, not you.

- **Say "no" despite the other person's disapproval**

The ability to say "no" despite somebody's objection is a solid demonstration. Individuals who can do this are present in reality. Because in reality, there is no way that we can accommodate all of their needs and wants. When this happens, they will become baffled, even disappointed. However, keep in mind that what they are feeling is part of human nature. Most of these individuals would then forgive and forget. Sound individuals realize that getting what you want all the time is not possible, even when the desires are genuine. In any case, when we cannot endure another person's mistake or objection, it ends up hard stating "no." It winds up more diligently for us to state it or have limits. Manipulators exploit this shortcoming and use dissatisfaction and objection in extraordinary structures to get us to do what they need.

- **Tolerate the other person's negative affect**

We can demonstrate compassion for people's pity, hurt, or even annoyance when accommodating them without needing to back down and reverse our decision. Keep in mind, a solid relationship is described by common minding, shared genuineness, and shared regard. If you are involved with somebody who uses manipulation and unhealthy control consistently, begin to see little propensities that may not be clear to you at first. As you are more grounded, you are better ready to endure how the other individual's negative impact on you is only bringing you down. Thus, this turns into a positive development that liberates you from their manipulative grasps. This will engender a complexity of sorts with the people in your life. The manipulator may start to withdraw and consider your time, your emotions, your wants, and your needs, or they will proceed onward to someone else who is an easy target of manipulation practices.

BASIC TRICKS USED BY MANIPULATORS

As soon as you have realized how knowledge of certain truths about yourself can enlighten you to notice manipulative tactics by other people, you will start to divulge from what you are to what a manipulator can do. With that in mind, if you wish to overcome manipulation, you need to be wary of the basic tactics used by manipulators. Once you have a firm grasp as to what you want and what you do not want, you can go head-to-head with a manipulator and even counter some of their most-used techniques. Nevertheless, always keep in mind that as soon as you realize that you are being manipulated, the manipulator loses. It is simply a matter of whether or not you wish to turn the tables and become the manipulator yourself.

- **Accusing your rival of what he is blaming you for**

This is often referred to as the act of pointing to another person's wrongdoing. When enduring an onslaught and experiencing difficulty regarding safeguarding themselves, manipulators tend to reverse the situation. They blame their rivals for committing the exact things that they are being blamed for. *"You state that I don't love you! I think it is you who does not cherish me!"*

• **Appealing to power**

Numerous individuals are in wonderment of those in power or authority, or those who have status. What's more intriguing is that there are various images to which individuals experience extraordinary dedication. Remember, those who are easily manipulated admire those who are in power. Moreover, those who are in power are aware of their ability to control others by never criticizing them. Instead, they use complex misleading tactics to maneuver their thoughts and alter their decision-making process.

Rabble-rousers that effectively control individuals realize that the vast majority are promptly deceived along with these statements. As a result, they collaborate with those in power. This entails the need to look for experts and other educated individuals that will support their perspectives or, at least, not criticize them.

Cigarette organizations once enlisted researchers who were arranged to state that there is not any confirmation that these products can cause lung disease; however, they knew that the proof was already there. Cigarette organizations additionally established The American Tobacco Foundation, a group of specialists trying to find the impacts of smoking on a person's wellbeing. However, in all actuality, the analysts were trying to shield the interests of the tobacco business under the pretense of a logical idea that smoking is not dangerous. They misled the public beguiling them into believing that they were speaking logically precautionary measures.

- **Appealing to encounter**

Nevertheless, this appeal to experience provides them with an image of someone who is capable; this may be used to attack their opponent's lack of experience, even though they have limited experiences. You can easily identify this manipulation tactic at times when someone is trying to distort their capabilities about a particular subject.

• **Appealing to fear**

People have fears. The unscrupulous manipulators realize a reality that individuals will, in general, respond crudely when any of these feelings of dread are enacted. Subsequently, they speak to themselves as being able to ensure individuals against these dangers, even when they are not capable of doing so. This is the same for when we talked about giving the target a glimpse of how their most desired outcome is achievable, without really providing it to them. Nonetheless, some politicians and legislators frequently utilize this methodology to ensure that individuals line up behind administrative experts and do what the legislature – that is, the thing that the government officials – need.

- **Appealing to sympathy**

Manipulators can depict themselves and their circumstances to the public in a means to make them feel frustrated about their current situation.

Utilization of this ploy empowers the manipulator to occupy consideration from those individuals who may be going through the same thing. Nevertheless, appealing to sympathy is a tactic that most politicians would use to redirect the attention of the public to matters that do not affect their demise.

- **Appealing to well-known interests**

Manipulators and tricksters are always mindful as to how they introduce themselves as persons who possess the right qualities and perspectives among the group of spectators, particularly, the sacred beliefs of the crowd. Everybody has a few partialities, and a great many people feel contempt toward a person or thing. Experts manipulators tend to stir up contempt and prejudices among the crowd.

They suggest that they concur with the group of spectators. They go about as though they have shared ideologies. They attempt to persuade the group of spectators that their enemy does not regard sacred the ideologies that they hold sacred. There is numerous potential in this technique. A particular technique named as the "Just Plain Folks Fallacy" is when an individual infers something along the lines of:

"It is comforting to be back in my home, and with people, I can truly trust. It's incredible to be with those who face things squarely; those who utilize their presence of mind to achieve things; individuals who don't have confidence in highfalutin methods for thinking and acting."

- **Appealing to confidence**

This technique is firmly identified with the past points; yet, it stresses what appears to have breezed through the trial of time. Individuals are regularly oppressed by the social traditions and standards of their way of life, just as social conventions. What is conventional to most tend to appear as if it is the correct decision? It is important to note that manipulators infer how they regard sacred the ideologies and beliefs that the group of spectators is familiar with. These individuals suggest that their enemy aims to obliterate the customs, as well as social conventions. Moreover, they do not stress over whether or not these conventions hurt guiltless individuals. They make the presence of being autonomous in the crowd's perspectives; yet, it would typically be the exact opposite thing. There is a realization that individuals are generally suspicious of the individuals who conflict with present social standards and built up conventions. They realize enough to stay away from these. As a result, there is a kind of restriction on how social traditions are unwittingly and carelessly bound.

- **Begging the inquiry**

One simple approach to demonstrate a point is to accept it in any case. Think about this model:

"Well, what type of government do you want, a government by liberal do-gooders that can shell out your hard-earned dollars or a government-controlled by business minds that knows how to live within a strict budget and generate jobs that put people to work?"

One minor departure from this error has been classified as "question-begging epithets," the utilization of expressions is a prejudgment of an issue by how it is allowed. In an instance, "Shall we defend freedom and democracy or cave into terrorism and tyranny?" Through the inquiry along these lines, we abstain from discussing awkward inquiries like: "Yet, would we say we are truly propelling human opportunity? Are we truly democratic or simply expanding our capacity, our control, our predominance, our access to foreign markets?" Keep in mind that the statements individuals utilize when bringing about the truth concerning an issue. There is the regular choosing of statements that surmise the accuracy of the situation on a particular issue.

· **Creating a false dilemma**

A genuine problem happens when we are compelled to pick between two similarly unsuitable choices. A false dilemma happens when we are convinced that we have just two, similarly inadmissible decisions, when we truly have multiple potential outcomes accessible to us. Think about the accompanying case: *"Either we will lose the war on terrorism, or we should surrender a portion of our traditional freedoms and rights."*

Individuals are frequently prepared to acknowledge a false dilemma since few are agreeable with the complex qualifications. Clearing absolutes is a part of their manipulative tactics. There is a need to have clear and basic decisions.

- **Hedging what you state**

Manipulators frequently hole up behind words, declining to submit themselves or give straightforward replies or answers. This enables them to withdraw at times of need. Whenever they are found forgetting data significant to the current situation, they would think of some other reason for not being able to come up with said information. At the end of the day, when forced, they may be able to give in; however, to be an excellent manipulator, you should renege on your missteps, conceal your mistakes, and gatekeep what you state at whatever point conceivable.

- **Oversimplifying the issue**

Since most people are uncomfortable at comprehending profound or unobtrusive contentions, some are fond of oversimplifying the issue to further their potential benefit. *"I couldn't care less what the measurements inform us concerning the purported abuse of detainees; the main problem is whether we will be tough on crime. Spare your compassion toward the criminals' victims, not for the actual criminals."* The reality being overlooked is that the maltreatment of criminals is a crime in itself. Tragically, individuals with an over-simple mindset could not care less about criminal conduct that victimizes criminals.

- **Raising only complaints**

Your adversary is giving valid justifications to acknowledge a contention; however, the truth of the matter is that your mind is made up and nothing can change it. Gifted manipulators would react with objections after objections. As their rivals answer one protest after another, they would proceed again to object and object. The implicit mentality of the manipulator is that *"regardless of what my rival says, I will continue to object because nothing else will convince me otherwise."*

- **Rewriting history**

The most noticeably awful acts and outrages tend to vanish from chronicled accounts while false dreams can be made to become facts. This phenomenon is often observed with Patriotic History. The composition of a contorted type of history is supported by the adoration of the nation and regularly defended by the charge of the antagonism. The truth of the matter is that our mind is persistently attempting to re-portray occasions of the past to absolve itself and denounce its spoilers. Chronicled composing frequently goes with the same pattern, particularly in the composition of reading material for schools. In this way, in recounting to an anecdote about what has happened, those who perform manipulative tactics do not hesitate to contort the past in the manners in which they accept they can pull off. As usual, the manipulator is prepared with self-justifying excuses.

- **Shifting the burden of proof**

This act alludes to when an individual has the obligation to demonstrate some of his declarations. A good example would be the instance that happened inside a court. The examiner possesses the obligation to prove guilt past distrust. Furthermore, the defense should not claim the responsibility of having to prove innocence. Those who are capable of manipulating others do not need to assume the weight of evidence for what they attest to. Along these lines, they harness the right tool in shifting the burden of proof to their rivals.

- **Talking in vague generalities and statements**

It is difficult to refute individuals when they cannot be bound. So, as opposed to concentrating on specifics, those who are capable of manipulating others tend to speak in the most unclear phrases that they can pull off. We have already talked about how certain statements and generalities can put another person in a daze, which makes it easier for them to be manipulated. This misrepresentation is well known for politicians. For instance, *"Overlook what the cowardly liberals say. It's the right time to be tough, to be hard on criminals, to punish terrorists, and be tough on those who disparage our nation."* Manipulators ensure they do not utilize particulars that may make individuals question what they are doing in the first place.

• Telling enormous falsehoods and big lies

The majority of the people are liars, even about the little things; yet, there is still a reluctance to say things other than the truth. In any case, these individuals realize that if you insist on a lit long enough, numerous individuals will trust you – particularly, on the off chance that you have the tools of mass media to broadcast a particular lie.

Every gifted manipulator is centered around what you can get individuals to accept, not on what is valid or false. They realize that the human personality does not normally look for reality; it looks for solace, security, individual affirmation, and personal stake.

Individuals regularly would prefer not to know the reality, particularly, certainties that are agonizing, that uncover their logical inconsistencies and irregularities, and that uncover what they hate about themselves or even their nation.

Some so many manipulators are exceptionally gifted in telling huge lies and, in this manner, causing those lies to appear valid.

CHAPTER 7: BODY - STATE CONTROL

Your body is the biggest piece of your unconscious mind and when you bring the body back into what we do, your changes happen faster, it's deeper and it doesn't matter what your listeners believe. It doesn't matter how much critical faculties are involved, the longer you get them engaged, the faster you overwrite their conscious critical faculty. You have to get your body involved.

No matter what situation or context we are in, if we can't control our state, if we can manage our psycho-emotional state, it doesn't matter what skills we have, it doesn't matter how much skills we have, it doesn't matter how much training we have. If we can't get into a state that allows us to access those resources we might as well not know them.

It's how we control our body states that determine the amplitude and the strength of the signals we send to another person's nervous system. It's not just about rapport, it's about how strong the signal we send is and the fastest way to do that is by changing our body states.

State control comes in two varieties:

1. Physiological

2. Volitional: Will power.

There is a saying and believe that you can't make people do things against their will, that is a lie because that will imply that people have a will to resist, most people do not especially in our modern times. Most people to muster any kind of will has to generate an emotional response, anger, desire, some kind of emotional response, to express, will power. Your will power is not an abstract concept it's based on two physiological phenomena or nutrients: blood sugar and sleep.

Your will power is based on the amount of blood sugar in your system and the amount of sleep you get. You burn up will power units, we call them self-regulating units; you have a finite amount. You burn them up anytime you have to exert control over your emotional states or your primal drives. When you run out of SRUs which are the functional units of your will power you will default to hedonistic, primal, unconscious behaviors.

We go through the day, and various things deplete our will power. We burn up our SRUs anytime we have to control ourselves, anytime we have to exert emotional control, anytime we have to quiet any kind of neurological arousal. One of the fastest ways to override the critical factor is intense emotion. Any form of emotion is neurological arousal, the higher the level of arousal in the nervous system, the faster your will power checks out.

As your day becomes more tasking, as you begin to deal with more stuff, you start to burn the tank at the end of the day you get home there's nothing left. Unconscious drives kick in, you start eating the cheesecake, drinking beer, watching internet porn, anything that gives you some kind of pleasure, hedonistic responses that relieve stress. Will power is a finite resource.

Will power can be trained. Special Forces, for example, are drilled to remain functional even in highly stressful situations.

Your will power will be the first thing to check out when you want to control your state because our emotional states are driven by our physiology.

3. FEEDBACK LOOPS

Let's say I have a sickness or condition in my liver I have to get medicine for. If I have a syringe full of medicine I can inject it into my arm, will it eventually get to my liver? Yes. If I inject it into my leg will it eventually get to my liver? Yes. If I inject it directly into my liver will it eventually get to my liver? Yes. What's the variable? Time; that is how long it takes.

Everything in the body works on a feedback loop. One of the most common ones we use in hypnosis is the *mind-body* feedback loop. The mind affects the body, the body affects the mind. We impose a strong enough change in one, it ends up affecting the other. A similar feedback loop exists between your physiology (in other words your posture) and your emotions.

Every emotional state that we generate has a corresponding posture and breathing rate. Every physiology that we take on or assume creates a specific emotional state. So we can use one to affect the other. Because most of what we do cognitively is generated organically (in the brain), anything that starts in the body tends to have more amplitude and push than what we just start with our thought. So while you can affect the body using the mind, it's easier to affect the mind using the body.

The mind-body feedback loop is important. There's another one that we use especially when we talk about rapport. In rapport, we have this concept we call Pacing and leading. When we pace someone, what we're doing is copying something that they're doing, feeling or experiencing; we're matching it or in some cases mirroring it. We're identifying something about them and doing it too. A lead is something we want someone else to do, experience or feel.

In the world of rapport building of pacing and leading, we have these two concepts called *matching and mirroring.*

If my friend John assumes certain physiology and I do the same thing, I am matching John. If John sticks his right hand in his ear and I also stick my right hand in my ear, then I'm matching him.

But if John sticks his left hand in his ear and I stick my right hand in my ear, I am now mirroring John. If John was looking at his reflection in the mirror, that's how he will see it. The difference in my experience is that mirroring tends to be more powerful, it signals sameness. When you mirror somebody properly your voice tends to sound like their internal dialogue and we never resist what we say to ourselves.

Some Masters of hypnosis will tell you that to get rapport with somebody, you should match and mirror them but there's another school of thought that says matching and mirroring is what you do after you build rapport. Have you ever noticed that when you connect with someone you automatically start doing what they do?

The truth is both are true. Rapport can generate matching and mirroring and matching and mirroring can generate rapport. But that's not good enough for me because rapport is going to happen anyway, whether you match and mirror or not. Because we live in a physical universe and in that physical universe we have laws. One of the primary laws of physics is the law of entrainment. If I take different clocks with swinging pendulums swinging at different rates and place them in a room all by themselves, eventually all the clocks will start swinging at the same frequency. Because anything that moves has a frequency and all frequencies seek harmony, they seek synchronization. The only variable is time.

Rapport must happen when two objects that have molecules that move are close together; you just have to recognize it when it happens. You have to remember the first language you ever learned, the language of the body, the language of feelings, which was your first language. It's that part of you that always seeks connection, the part of you that you've forgotten because the school system, religion, the government, television, movies, books have taken your mind somewhere else.

If you want to become more fully human, you have to get back into your body, you have to become more self-aware and when you do, magic happens. But it's not magic exactly, it's science. Because the most powerful rhythmic source in the body is the human heart. Your heart in addition to being the most powerful rhythmic source in your body radiates an electromagnetic field 8 feet in diameter that can be measured from the body.

Our energy fields intersect when we are close together. When we take that concept from the entrainment principle into the field of organic interaction we call *coherence*. It's a deeper level of rapport; it's neurological where our heartbeats can synchronize. The human heart is autonomous, it's directly connected to the brain and it sends more information to the brain than the brain sends to the heart. Not metaphysics, neuroscience.

If we can learn to interact with the system at a physiological level, we can learn to get back to our feelings and regulate the system. We can influence anyone, pretty much from anywhere; start with how we use our bodies.

CHAPTER 8: MANIPULATING THE MIND THROUGH NLP

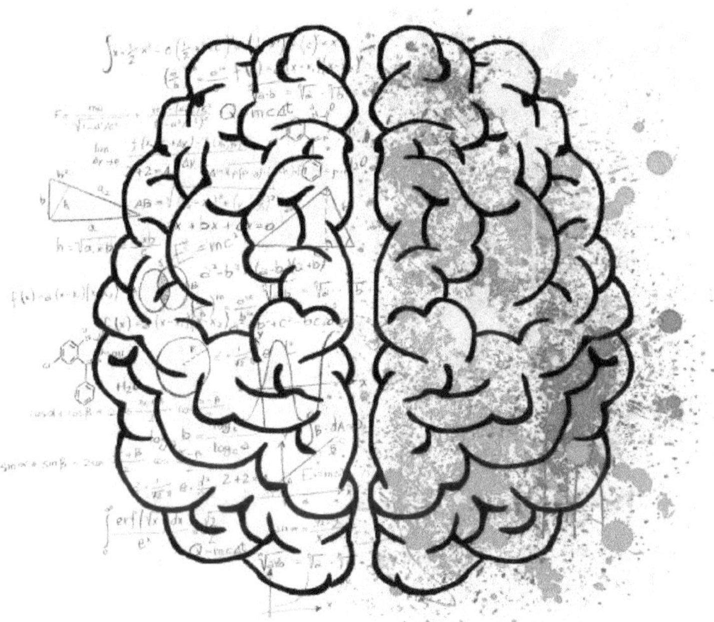

NLP, THE MIND, AND ULTIMATE CONTROL

Have you ever wondered how some people can handle change constructively and creatively? While some people are knocked off balance by changes in their lives, others seem to fit right in perfectly. Why is it that some people seem to be in the right place at the right time? How come some people have good relationships while others cannot get it together even for a week? Is there some form of good luck or inborn traits, making some people more successful than others?

One of the professors at the University of California called John Grinder, and his student called Richard Bandler started to work on a behavioral study project in the 1970s. They observed the behaviors of successful people and were more interested in why some people so good at what they do when compared to others. The findings helped them to develop the neurolinguistics programming, which involved observing, codifying, and replicating the behaviors and thought patterns of successful people. The programming explores the relationship between our neuro (how we think) linguistic (how we communicate) and programs (pour patterns of emotions and behaviors).

The background of Neuro-linguistic programming is that positive behaviors that lead to success can be copied. The professor and the student were interested in the difference between the thought patterns, behaviors, and language use of successful and unsuccessful people. Their findings are the basis of NLP today. Simply put, the researchers claimed that success has very little to do with luck. You do not have to be lucky to succeed. Changing your approaches to life can help you to become more successful in relationships, career, social spec, and other situations. Though some people develop natural ways of becoming successful, these ways of thinking, acting, and speaking can be learned by anyone who is willing to give it a shot.

The Neurolinguistics programming was developed years ago, but a lot of redefinition has taken place over the years. Currently, NLP has become a commonly used technique in self-development and therapy. It is used in education, business, military, and above all, for individuals. NLP can be successfully applied in personal life, and a lot of big companies train their staff on how to use NLP with clients.

NLP is about how we develop mental representations sounds, images, and verbal descriptions of different situations. When we become aware of the internal maps of reality within us, it becomes easier to consciously change our inner landscape and consequently respond differently to people and situations in the outside world.

One of the main benefits of using NLP is that results can be seen very quickly. For instance, people with some kinds of phobias can be treated in a matter of minutes using some of the techniques found in NLP. Further, blockages and fears can be dealt with easily and quickly through the use of NLP. Honestly speaking, NLP has shed a lot of light on how we interact with our physical and social environments and other aspects of life.

NLP, MANIPULATION, AND MIND CONTROL

Can NLP help you avoid negative manipulation and mind control? Yes, NLP can help anyone to fight manipulators. Often, we move along life on autopilot- responding to life in an extensively automatic way. This leaves us vulnerable to manipulation because we hardly analyze situations critically and make strong decisions. When living life on autopilot, we tend to follow what other people are doing (social proof) and also allow other people to influence our choices. Sometimes go through life drive by those subconscious programs which we have learned and practiced for years – some of them we practice since childhood.

Some self-development advocates and personal change ambassadors can fail to explain to us how we can avoid the specific tools we should apply to improve our lives. On the other hand, NLP lays out the tools you need to implement that change. It informs you that you are responsible for your actions, reactions, and responses to the situations in life. NLP allows you to get behind the steering wheel and take charge of your life instead of having another person drive you around.

NLP is practiced more because of its practicality – The tools are functional, and a wide range of challenges can be addressed through NLP. Some of the issues include;

• Developing better relationships,

- Becoming more healthy

- Overcoming phobias and fears such as fear of public

speaking,

- Improving communication

- Being more successful and impactful in your career and

family life.

Success in any field of life, be it career, sport, family, et cetera requires excellence. Neuro-linguistic programming is a roadmap for this excellence. Although other factors like luck and innate ability play a role in the success of an individual, the majority of NLP tools must be applied. Success is a predictable result of behaving and thinking in a certain way.

CHAPTER 9: INTERPRETING VERBAL COMMUNICATION

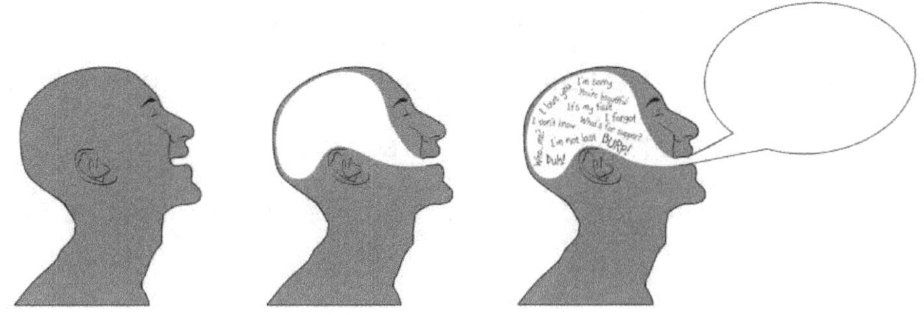

In this chapter, we are going to take a close look at how verbal communication comes into play when dealing with interpersonal communication. These ideas will help you focus on how your voice and the words you say can convey a certain message.

The most common means of communication is verbally, usually through speaking. What this means is that, as humans, we use our voice to produce sounds. These sounds are then decoded by the brain and meaning is attached to them. If a sound does not have meaning attached to it, then it is essentially gibberish.

This is the foundation of language. Language is a collection of sounds and symbols, which have meaning attached to them, and are then decoded by a special system learned over time. Each language is a collection of systems used to identify the meaning of these sounds. So, the English language is a system in which sounds are interpreted by the brain and decoded to decipher meaning.

Language is so complex that it takes children many years of training and schooling to get the fundamentals of the language down. Then, it takes even longer for a person to fully master a language. There are master's degrees and PhDs focused on individual languages. That is how vast a field of knowledge a single language can be.

Now, it should be noted that language has a written dimension and an oral one. In this chapter, we will be focusing on the oral dimension of language as written communication is not part of the scope that pertains to this book. While it is a fascinating field, understanding written communication requires a completely different approach which will divert our attention for the main topic of this book.

So, oral communication is the primary means by which humans communicate. Even a newborn uses oral communication to send a message as to what they are feeling. For example, a baby will use crying as a signal to their caregiver that they are in distress. Naturally, that distress can range from being hungry to a poopy diaper. Nevertheless, even a newborn child can use verbal communication to convey meaning.

As an individual can grow and develop their cognitive skills, language becomes the primary focus of learning. While other areas of learning such as math and reading skills are vitally important, much of the focus of primary schooling is placed on learning to speak properly. What speaking properly does is that it provides a child, and future adult, the tools to better express themselves and convey the meaning they want to share with others around them.

That is why language becomes the principal vehicle by which oral communication takes place. Sounds and utterances are given meaning. These meanings are learned and quickly put to the test. When other people understand these sounds, then communication takes place. If for some reason, these sounds are not decoded effectively, communication breaks down.

This point regarding sounds and their decoding is the underpinning of oral communication.

How so?

Think about the old adage: it's not what you say, but how you say it.

The meaning you convey in your oral communication will inextricably depend on the tone, the pitch and even timbre of your voice. If you pay attention to these aspects, you will be able to figure out how crucial getting a proper handle on your voice can be.

One classic example is raising your voice.

When you raise your voice, what are you signaling to your interlocutor?

If you have a disagreement, raising your voice can be taken as a sign of an escalating interaction. It can also be taken as a sign of aggression to which your counterpart may choose to take a defensive position. This may lead to conflict if not handled appropriately.

Conversely, raising your voice can be taken as a warning of impending danger. For instance, if you yell, "watch out" those around you will hardly think you are showing aggression. Quite the opposite, they will assume a defensive position as a response to the danger which you have indicated.

These subtle nuances are learned over years and years of practice. Children are not instinctively born with these skills. That is why they are taught in school. Children must be trained in these aspects so that they can fit in properly within their social context.

Master coaches and trainers have developed courses and programs in which they train their students on how to master their voices to get the right message across. Television newscasters and radio personalities must go through some type of training so that they can be effective communicators. Otherwise, they may inadvertently commit errors when broadcasting.

The most common training that newscaster goes through is accent neutralization. While there is nothing wrong with a person's native accent, the inflections of such accents may not be universally known to all potential audiences. Consequently, accent training is needed to have a flat, neutral tone that can be more easily understood by anyone who tunes in.

With that in mind, let's take a look at the various aspects that go into oral communication. By becoming keenly aware of these aspects, you can manipulate your tone of voice to suit your communication needs. In particular, you can modulate your voice to suit the occasion and situation you are in. After all, it is one thing to speak at a funeral while it is an entirely different ballgame if you are giving a sales pitch.

The first aspect that we are going to be taking a look at is tone.

The tone of voice is perhaps the single-most-important element when it comes to verbal communication. By the same token, a lower tone of voice can signal that you are sharing confidential information or that you do not want others to hear what you are saying.

Besides, a lower tone of voice may signal a calm and peaceful tone especially when you are trying to diffuse a situation. For instance, if there is an escalation in your counterpart's tone of voice, you can counter with a flat and even tone. While you are hardly backing down, all your doing is putting a stop to the escalation of the confrontation.

Using an even tone is very helpful when you are doing a presentation or giving a speech. While most coaches will tell you that you need to show emotion (which is partially true), maintaining an even tone will signal to your audience that you are in control, that is, you know what you are talking about.

In terms of showing emotion, especially if you are doing a sales pitch, it is worth mentioning that you can play with the pitch in your voice.

Pitch refers to a higher or lower register in your voice. You can play with the pitch in your voice regardless of whether you have a squeaky voice or whether you sound like Darth Vader. The fact is that you can use pitch to indicate your emotions.

For instance, you would consider using a lower pitch when you are delivering a somber address or speaking at a funeral. In contrast, you can use a higher pitch when you are doing a sales presentation or giving good news.

Hence, pitch plays an important role in conveying emotion. Of course, you want to be careful that you don't overdo it. Most folks tend to go a bit over the top and speak with a high and squeaky voice when they get excited. Furthermore, some folks speak in a monotone despite being in the middle of a festive environment. In such cases, these people are seen as dull and boring. So, it is important to make sense of where you are and what the situation may dictate.

Along with the pitch, intonation plays a great deal of importance on communicating information. Intonation comes in two main variants, rising and falling. As such, you can use rising or falling intonation depending on the situation you find yourself in.

In general terms, rising intonation is used to elicit a response, that is when asking a question. Now, the grammar behind questions varies from language to language. Nevertheless, most languages using rising intonation on the tail end of a sentence to signal that you need a response.

For example, "do you want something to drink?" would sound something like this, "do you want something to DRINK?" The caps indicate that the word "drink" has a rising intonation thereby indicating that your counterpart needs to respond.

Falling intonation is used to indicate that you are done talking. This signals your interlocutor that they are free to participate. If you don't provide an appropriate signal that you are done talking, you will leave your counterpart hanging. They may become confused because they won't be clear on whether you are done talking or you have more to say.

For instance, a statement such as, "let's go to the movies" ought to end with falling intonation since you are done speaking. Then, your interlocutor would respond accordingly. By the same token, you counterpart will use falling intonation in the answer to signal that they agree or disagree.

However, your interlocutor may respond to this statement with a question like, "now?" In this case, your counterpart needs to know if you are leaving at the time of speaking or later on. What this does is that it provides you with the option of replying or not. Naturally, these interactions all seem perfectly normal. Yet, they may confuse speakers of languages that do not follow similar patterns. Hence, understanding these non-linguistic clues are vital to engaging in successful communication.

CHAPTER 10: YOU HAVE THE ADVANTAGE, LEARN HOW TO EXPLOIT THAT

As with any new thing that you are trying to do and the techniques that you are going to learn from that, there is going to be a kind of learning curve along the way. you will be able to look at some insight into some of the typical stages of progress that occur when someone is learning dark NLP for the first time. Each of the different stages of progress will clearly be described out to you, and then you will have the advice that is needed in order to progress to the ultimate aim of dark NLP, which is to become a constant predator.

To start with is the first stage of dark NLP. This first stage is often known as a tentative form of exploration. During this stage, someone who has heard about the dark NLP and some of the unique ways that it can change your perspective on life and the world will begin to consider its ideas and then can weigh these new ideas against some of their perceptions of the world.

When you reach this point, it is possible for the person not to agree with the ideas of dark NLP, they may agree with some of the parts but not all of them, or they may decide that they agree with the ideas that come with dark NLP. These individuals are merely judging them in light of the experience that they have. To help the individual go beyond this kind of phase, it is advised that you actively seek to apply your understanding of dark NLP to the world around you.

After you have spent a little bit of time looking at dark NLP and some of the basics that come with it, and you have had some time to see whether the ideas are a good match with your own personally views of reality, you may agree that there is at least the potential of dark NLP to be useful. This is the stage of the process that is often known as cautious acceptance. It is during this time that you will start using the lens of dark NLP, but it still takes some conscious effort to look at the world in that manner. You may even start to question your understanding of morality when you are in this part.

The next thing that you want to work on is figuring out how to push beyond the cautious acceptance. You can do this by making a conscious effort to put some of the techniques of dark NLP to the motion. You will want to specifically pay attention to any of the techniques that are related to influencing yourself, as well as others, as fast as you can. You will find that through more experience and practice, and for seeing personal success, using a technique, you will find that it is easier to accept these techniques in your life.

Following the cautious acceptance that we talked about above, you will then need to progress to a new level of using dark NLP that is going to be known as casual competence. When you are at this stage, you will stop having to put in so much effort to use the dark NLP techniques. You will start to naturally think in terms of dark NLP concepts, and over time, it is going to require progressively less effort on your part. You may even find that you are able to use the ideas of dark NLP to take control over your own life and to make sure that you can influence others near you, without even having to think about it.

The biggest distinction that comes with this is that once you reach this stage, it is going to show that you are to a new level of progress. You will know it has happened when you realize that you have gained some influence over others, and when you realize this, there isn't a level of guilt that comes with it.

To make sure that you are able to get the most out of this stage, it is important to begin to put it into practice, and to make sure that you track down the patterns that you see with your success. You may find that at this stage of your progress, you are going to benefit from keeping a journal so that you can keep track of the different routines that you do, and what happens to work well for your success. You stand the best chance of moving past this particular stage if you can learn how to identify the difference between those times when you are successful, and the times you are not.

We can then move on to the level that is beyond casual competence. These are all going to involve a good mastery of Dark NLP, one that can take a long time to reach and succeed at. There are no longer so many levels that are distinct when it comes to progress as there are gradual degrees of improvement. Signs that someone has gotten to this stage of dark NLP is going to include many things such as the ability to read the power balance no matter what situation you are in, the ability to mirror the other person without even thinking about it, and even how to influence the other person with some deep and artificial rapport, without all the effort.

The mastery that you have of dark NLP is going to be reliant on how willing you are to absorb some of the concepts and techniques that are described in this guidebook. To make this happen, you need to be willing and able to take some big actions in your life to get the right influence with dark NLP. You also need to be willing to figure out what patterns are going to lead you to success, and then use this to reach the next level of your mastery in the shortest space of time as possible.

As you are looking through your feelings and your emotions, you will come to a part that your mind is going to automatically think in terms of the concepts that are important to dark NLP. Once this happens, you will be able to interact with someone in a way that is going to force some rapport with them before exploiting them for your own needs. This means that you have gotten to the ultimate goal that comes with dark NLP, which means that you are now a constant predator.

A PERSONAL SWOT

The next thing that we need to take a look at here is known as a personal SWOT. This is an acronym that is going to talk about strengths, weaknesses, opportunities, and threats. This is a tool that a lot of different businesses like to work with to help them come up with marketing campaigns and to ensure that they are going to beat out the competition.

But you can create one for your own use that is going to provide insight into the different positive and negative aspects of a person.

So, how do you go through this and make it work for yourself? The first thing that you should ask yourself is to figure out what your main strengths are, and your main weaknesses. You may want to go through and jot down a list of the things that you see as strengths and weaknesses. The order doesn't matter here, you just want to make sure that it is as complete as possible.

After you have had some time to write down all of the different aspects that fit into these two categories that you can, you can then narrow them down. This analysis is going to take way too long if you have to sort through twenty or more things for example. Pick out the top five things that you can begin to work on and then rank them. This gives you a look at the view of your major weaknesses and strengths and we can work from there.

After you take some time to find your strengths and weaknesses, which are basically the view that you have with your inner self at the time, then it is important to analyze the range of possible opportunities that are going to exist inside your life right now, and any threats that could cause a disruption to the current way of life that you have.

Now, one of the things that you need to remember about here is that your weaknesses are not something that should be seen in a negative light here. Your weaknesses here are areas where there is a lot of chances for you to improve things. Let's say that three of the personal weaknesses that you want to focus on will include bad presentation skills, limited social life, and a low amount of confidence when you speak out in public. Instead of looking at these like weaknesses, you can look at them more like a puzzle that you need to spend some time-solving. Once you are able to solve the puzzle and get all of the pieces to work together, you will be able to solve those weaknesses and get them to work for you.

You can use the information that you get in the SWOT to work with several of the techniques of dark NLP, such as choosing your habits, influencing others, and envisioning your future.

BREAKING THE RAPPORT

Up to this point, we have spent a lot of time talking about the different ways that you can build up some rapport with the other person, making sure that they are soft to your influence. Now we need to take a moment to learn the best way to break this rapport, and then build it back up over some time.

Before you are able to take control over another person by breaking the rapport, you must come up with a solid level of rapport. You then need to make sure that you reach the stage o influence where you can lead the body language of the other person you are interacting with. Once you have reached this level, then you are ready to begin the process of breaking the rapport tactically.

To break the rapport with the other person, it is time to stop mirroring them. Switch over to a brusque and negative tone of voice and do anything that is going to seem like you are trying to get away from the rapport. You will know that this is successful because the other person in the conversation is going to start acting like they are dejected or confused.

First, the other person is going to feel like there was some kind of loss that happened because all of the good emotions that you sent their way will be gone. Second, you are going to trigger the natural inclination of the other person to chase after and seek your validation to fill up the void of your approval.

Of course, once you are successful at breaking the rapport with the other person, you do still allow them a chance to regain the rapport again. The timing of this is going to need to be strategic in the way that you can reward the desired behavior or statement of the other person before you give in. for example, if the other person is trying to regain the rapport with you and they touch you, and you want them to repeat this, you would then reconnect rapport with them at that time. they would make the link of good feelings of the rapport with this behavior and repeat it in the future.

You will find that breaking the rapport that you have built up with the other person can be a really powerful tool, and it is one that you should use sparingly. It is often best to deploy it to make sure that there is sometimes the element of chase and tension in the interaction and to help with the emotional progress that you are building. It is possible to build and break the rapport a few times in the same communication but do be careful about overdoing it. The more that you do this, the harder it is going to be to rebuild that deep rapport and if you push it too much, then you are going to make it so that the person isn't even interested in you anymore.

CONNECTIONS AND ASSOCIATIONS

Let's think back to those neural pathways. The brain has billions of neurons and trillions of connections. Our memories are made through our infinite neural connections, and our ability to recall information comes from those neural connections. When we form a neural connection in our brain, we create a channel or highway for that same bit of information to travel every time you think of that same thought. This is how thought patterns can get created. When you are used to utilizing the same thought patterns and processes all the time, you strengthen those neural pathways, making them more available and more deeply connected and rooted in your brain function.

When we form habits, whether they are good or bad, we are concentrating on the same thought function, even when it is an unconscious habit, and many habits are unconscious thought processes. The same thought function repeated multiple times a day, many times a week, often over a year, will continue to stimulate and deepen the neural pathway associated with that thought pattern.

So, let's put it into an example. Every time you make a mistake while practicing the piano, in your head, you think the word "stupid." Your brain begins to form a neural pathway and connection to you playing the piano and the feeling of stupidity. As you continue to practice and make mistakes, you continue to reinforce the word stupid for making mistakes while learning the piano. Eventually, the more you practice, the more mistakes you make because your brain is already programmed to think 'stupid' if you fumble at all. As this feeling becomes stronger, you become less interested in playing the piano because it just makes you feel dumb and you would rather be doing something that didn't make you feel that way.

Your brain was able, in a short space of time, to associate learning the piano with feelings of stupidity causing you to eventually give up playing because you'd prefer not to feel that way. Why did you make that connection? Why did you label your mistake as stupid? Most likely, from an association or connection to something else, another thought pattern, or learned behavior. It may have come from a strict instructor whose demand for perfection caused you to doubt your ability. It might have come from an earlier life experience that taught you that making mistakes is unacceptable.

Regardless of the root cause, it exists in all the neural channels in the mind and if repeated enough can become a thought pattern that will extend into our beliefs about ourselves.

We associate everything we know with what we have already learned and experienced, and what we are learning at the moment. Our entire experience can be based on connections and associations made in our minds.

If your mind is always making connections and associations, don't you think that you can change whatever negative thoughts you have to become more positive? Remember, the mind is malleable, flexible, and capable of change.

MIND MAPS AND FILTERS

MIND MAP

Every connection and association you make in your daily life experience becomes a part of your map. If you have never seen images of neurons in the brain, they look like a starburst or an egg that has been cracked on a pan and has many branches coming off of it. These branches form and the intricate neural highway that puts together all of the information you need to store and utilize your experience of life.

If you drive a car, then you have probably looked at a road atlas; it covers a massive territory, the whole country, even, and is built up of significant highways, roads, and landmarks. Your mind similarly maps your journey. You won't see roads and highways, but you will relate to your sensory experiences as part of this life atlas.

Mind maps are impressions of reality based on our senses and how they inform our experience of life. They are selective, with the ability to leave out many pieces of information to present the most clear-cut representation of your current reality or life territory. Whatever map you make is based on what it is that you notice or whatever it is you want to change.

Our map of reality is unique to us. No other human being on the planet has the same map that you do.

FILTERS

In addition to having your own, unique mind map, you also have filters. Filters act to determine what sort of world we live in; a sieve for our perceptions of reality. If your filters are in alignment with qualities of excellence, then you will go through the world looking for it; if your filters are in alignment with seeing problems in everything, then that is what you will find.

If you have a lot of limiting beliefs due to negative thought patterns, beliefs, and perceptions, then the world will be lacking for you. The same world can be full of beauty and opportunity, depending on how you choose to filter.

The language we use acts as a filter. Every unique person will have a completely different feeling about a word like "sunset." Every person's map has a different sensory experience of a sunset.

Beliefs are filters, too. What you believe to be true, will certainly influence your outlook and how you behave.

NLP is a filter, as well; it is a system that doesn't require that you change your values or beliefs, but that you approach life with a desire to experiment and a spirit of curiosity. It's just a model for excellence, but doesn't claim any objective truth: you are unique and cannot be generalized, but these tools and techniques are a filter, none the less.

BASIC NLP FILTERS

NLP breaks these filters into what it calls *frames*. There are five behavioral frames in NLP. They are:

First Frame = outcomes rather than problems

This can also be called the "blame frame." Focusing on problems rather than outcomes leads you to question "why do I have this problem," instead of "how can I change this to make it better."

Second Frame = how rather than why

Asking "how" instead of "why" will give you an understanding of the structure of a problem. If you just keep asking "why" you won't get closer to the "how" of solving the issues.

Third Frame = feedback rather than failure

In NLP, we say "there is no failure, only results." Failure is just a word to describe getting a result that you didn't want which gives you feedback for getting the results that you do.

Fourth Frame = possibilities rather than necessities

When you see something is possible, it shifts your focus. Fixating on a necessity leaves little room for expansion. We all have necessities, but if we adhere to a limited reality, we miss all of the opportunities that possibilities offer.

Fifth Frame = curiosity and fascination rather than assumptions

Any approach to learning new things and opening up to making change requires some curiosity and interest. When you only make assumptions, you strictly filter your reality, disallowing a more rational experience.

The map of your life is a colorful mural of all of the experiences of your life through your senses. You continue to build upon it every day and when you learn NLP tools, you give yourself new highways to drive on that lead to the path of excellence.

CHAPTER 11: PROS AND CONS OF PERSUASION AND MIND CONTROL

PERSUASION

Persuasion attempts to affect the victim's beliefs, intents, attitudes, motivations, and behaviors at large. It can as well be interpreted as a tool used by persuaders in search of personal advantages, for example, politics. Persuaders often use their resources to influence their victims. How the victim behaves is affected by the manipulator's threats, mostly verbal, and the personal physiological factors of the victim. Just like manipulation, persuasion involves several tactics, and they are as follows:

Use of force: In persuasion, there consists of the use of force when making demands, which makes it less practical to the letdown of the less unswerving way of coercion. The persuader gives no options; it is either the victim grants whatever is demanded or they must face the threats.

Machiavellianism: This tactic uses more of the manipulative techniques together with trickery to influence the victim. Persuaders influence the victims to be rich and get power.

Weapons of influence: This involves the following factors:

- *Reciprocity*: Reciprocity means that, when given something, you should try and repay in kind, too. This brings about a sense of obligation, which provides room for persuasion. Reciprocity instills the feeling of responsibility to the victim. It can lead to exchanges that are not equal.

- *Commitment and consistency*: When talking about the pros of persuasion, this is one of the critical aspects of wheedling as it is even embraced in society. It leads to better daily lives and gives way through the complex nature of contemporary life. Consistency helps in effective decision-making as it involves obeying and fulfilling a commitment. Commitment to a stance makes the committer involve themselves in self-persuasion, giving explanations in support of their obligations as a way of avoiding conflict.

- *Social proof*: This is acting to please people, or being influenced by what the surrounding people are doing and wanting to be like them. It involves the need to know what everyone else is doing, and is brought about by 'the influence of the crowd'. The issue about role models can turn out to be persuasive since the victim enjoys seeing similarities between them and their role models, hence, acting like them.

- *Likeness*: There will always be a 'yes' to a request from the people you like. Their physical beauty and similarity. Beautiful people get what they want quickly as their beauty comes with other favorable traits that may be attached to the attractiveness, such as being kind, talented, or intelligent.

- *Authority*: There is a common belief that experts do not lie as people listen and trust those who are knowledgeable. People who are at top authorities direct people to bring harm to others.

- *Scarcity*: Something scarce is assigned more value. This tactic is used by the marketers when convincing the customers to buy a specific product that serves the same purpose as the scarce one. When the victims see another much available product, they tend not to buy it; as they still want the limited product.

Having this said, the persuader thus needs to note that persuasion does not aim at defeating others, but rather winning over others. For successful persuasion, the persuader needs to analyze the situation, objectives, and the problems likely to be faced. After surveying, the persuader should confront the five obstacles; relations, credibility, communication mismatches, opinions, likes, and wants. Use presentation skills to make the pitch, then lastly safeguard the longtime success of any effective decision. To secure the commitments, the persuader tries politics since it is essential for personal benefits.

MIND CONTROL

On the other hand, mind control can as well be referred to as manipulating, thoughts restructuring, conditioning, cerebral regulation, intimidating influence and control, and the malicious use of set underlying forces, among many other names. The presence of more than one meaning means there is no agreement on the specific meaning of mind control. To be on the safe side, it can be referred to as changing people's habits and beliefs. Mind control falls under the influence and persuasion sectors. Influencing through mind control cannot be termed as fully manipulating someone but can be referred to as a continuum.

There are also other forms of forces that damage the target's identity and interfere with their decision-making ability. Undermind control, there are destructive sects and destructive cults. These are the forms of influence that use trickery and mind control techniques to benefit from the victim's weaknesses and satisfy the demands of the persuaders and cult leaders. Most of the intimate relationships are based on mind control mechanisms. For instance, a wife/hubby, preacher/member of the congregation, or even a psychotherapist/client kind of relationship could fit into this category.

Mind control thus refers to a structure of influences that meaningfully interrupt a target at the level of their individuality, generating a different pseudo-personality. It can also refer to the process of compromising a person's collective autonomy of decision and deeds. These compromises are made by agents that either change or interfere with the awareness, inspirations, behavioral consequences, and influences.

The manipulator creates dependency on the victims, makes decisions for them, and makes the victims feel like they are autonomous in their decision-making. The target of mind control is never aware that the manipulator is influencing them; neither are the victims informed of the consequences of the influence in their behavior.

During mind control, the following should be noted:

- *Mind control is a process* – controlling of the victim does not happen instantly. Though it takes time, the time length depends on aspects such as the method of mind control used, the manipulator's skills, how long the manipulator has been manipulating someone, and social as well as personal elements.

- *There is force involved in mind control* – the physical strength might be experienced, but there must be psychological and social forces.

There is a dissimilarity amid mind-controlling as well as indoctrination. In an indoctrination case, the target is aware that the manipulator is a rival. The victim is always pressured via physical forces, to behave in a manner that the victim would not normally act. But when the victim happens to escape from the manipulator's hands, the impacts of the brainwashing frequently vanish.

In a mind control case, the manipulator is always considered as a friend, and that means the victim does not normally try to defend themselves. At times, the victim cooperates because of the manipulator's 'sweet interests.' Coercion only distorts the victim's behavior, but mind control changes the attitudes, thoughts, practice, and the beliefs of the victim. Recognizing a mind control effect is hard since the victims never question their decisions as they think that whatever they decided on is what's best for them.

The victims don't think they can be manipulated by their friends. You should note that every manipulator uses the phrase, 'no one is holding a gun to your head.' This makes it difficult for the victim to argue with the manipulator. It also assures the victim that they have made the decision themselves, and no one has influenced them. The victim already knows that decisions made by oneself last longer and are always more powerful. Therefore, the victim is propelled into the more profound authenticity influenced by way of awareness controlling.

Which people then practice mind control? Which people wake up and go ahead to destroy other people's lives for their own benefits? The answer to this question is psychopaths and narcissists. Manipulative women or men who use mind control have no ethics. In society, the term 'manipulator' is not common as they are referred to as abusive wives or husbands, jealous boyfriend or girlfriends, strict bosses, or even controlling preachers. You should not fall for the myth that only the weak or vulnerable people are prone to mind control.

Those who claim they cannot be manipulated are actually the easiest to manage since they are never on the lookout for them. People do not wake up and plan on joining sects, but they get enrolled since getting subjected to mind control makes you comprehend better the way cults work, and the techniques used in these cults for attracting or keeping participants.

There are six principles of influence that are the weapons of influence in mind control. These principles work in EVERY society in the whole world, and they help a particular community to grow and be stable. They are called 'influencing weaponries' since their function is altering the mindfulness of the victims. It is because of this reason that a cult mediator rides on the coat-tails to persuade and manipulate the followers. The principles include:

- Mutuality

- Obligation and reliability

- Societal evidence

- Congeniality

- Power

- Insufficiency

Some cults use harmful mind control tactics to influence their members. They tend to change the member's identity through control of their behaviors, control their feelings, points of view, and by confining access to information. The victim's identity is changed because they are not aware that the manipulator is controlling them, their time, as well as their surroundings, are under control, fear is instilled in them, there is repression of the prior behaviors and attitudes, and new ones are introduced, and the victims are given a doctrine which bears an enclosed logic.

Mind control can be harmful or helpful, depending on the following factors.

- Techniques used by the manipulator

- The number of mind control techniques that are used.

- Whether there are cases of hypnosis.

- The manipulator's skills.

- The relationship between the victim and the cult leader, that is, how closely they are related.

- Instances of sexual abuse.

- Family and friend's support of the victim

People who have suffered mind control will always grow beliefs that help them deal with this situation. The victim's critical thinking is similarly repressed; that is why they constantly argue to keep their belief structures unbroken. The victims have been brainwashed to have some unprecedented beliefs like they can save the world, and they belong to elite groups, with exceptional bits of data that when properly used can transform all God's creatures.

PROS AND CONS

Many people think that persuasion and mind control are always evil actions and should be forbidden. Brainwashing strategies are being abused by various groups of people and even organizations in society. Everyone needs to be literate and understand how mind control techniques work, then incorporate it together with persuasion in their lives.

PROS

- In the contemporary world, everyone uses persuasion or mind control in various ways, either consciously or unconsciously. They are the best ways to communicate, especially among youths.

- Persuasion helps you get what you want in a simple way, without so much struggle.

- Being a persuader or being familiar with persuasion and mind control helps avoid getting manipulated, persuaded, or mind-controlled by manipulators, persuaders, or even cult leaders.

- Good mastering of persuasion and mind control tactics can make people have great sales. This is through overcoming buyer resistance. A salesperson tries all they can to show the customer that they empathize with the hardship of the purchase choice. Customers end up purchasing a product to satisfy the salesperson rather than themselves.

- Effective use of persuasion can lead to promotions or better work positions in workplaces.

- Being persuasive leads to making reasonable arguments based on facts, and this improves self-expression. Defense against an opposing group requires points to proving that the opposition is wrong and this makes the persuader share valid information.

- Persuasion and mind control improves employer-employee relationships as discussing with workers about any layoffs, benefits, an increase of premiums, and any other decisions that need to be made in the organization need effective persuasion. The employer tries to persuade the workers through logic, facts, and the assumption that the workers are paying attention emotionally without analyzing the situation deeply.

- For effective persuasion and mind control, there must be honesty and openness. Inducement does not involve trickery but rather provides the victim with facts that they can use to support their decisions. This can improve job performance and also increase self-esteem.

- Though persuasion is a common psychological mechanism used to influence people, mind control is more powerful and precise. This is one of the pros of mind control; powerful and efficiency.

- Mind control gives room to appeal to the victim's hearts more than their minds. This is important as anyone who has mind control skills can do anything that can be done by the rich or powerful, that is if the manipulator or persuader is poor.

- If used for personal benefits, mind control tactics can help one forget the practical challenges as they help refresh the mind.

CONS

- When used in politics, persuasion and mind control does not benefit a country anymore. It only succors to certain groups of people.

- Persuasion and mind control are used to conceal certain truths. Therefore, making issues seem different from what they are in a real sense. This promotes evil deeds and makes poor people appear high.

- Persuasion and mind control are used by more prominent organizations to deceive people into purchasing products that are not great for them and might lead to customers getting hooked or addicted to certain products. This benefits the organization or firms involved yet exploits the clients.

- Once used by parents on their children, persuasion and mind control hijacks whatever goes in the mind of these young ones. The parents might mislead their children by persuading them to either adopt new study methods, correct conduct, or even doing homework in certain ways. Children grow up thinking this is the only way to do things.

- It might lead to psychological harm to the victim.

- These techniques destroy relationships between friends, family, or significant others.

- An in-depth focus on persuasion and mind control can make the persuader forget about the victims' natural behavior. It can turn out to be overly suspicious.

CHAPTER 12: INFLUENCING THOSE AROUND YOU

"Never underestimate the influence you have on others."

-Laurie Buchanan Life Coach, Author

In addition to the tactful application of metaphors, modeling, anchoring, and reframing, there are a few more cardinal rules you should know about the art of influence and persuasion. Four more acts of persuasion are yours to be learned, practiced, and mastered. You've seen briefly that there's an influence to be had, just by being a good listener. In this section, we'll take a closer look at the power of listening and smiling. Similarly, we'll examine the use of vulnerability, forgiveness, and empathy as a means of persuasion and manipulation. This will be another layer of technique to place upon the skills you've already learned. By doing this, you're refining and sharpening your skills of persuasion.

THE ASSET OF LISTENING

Listening can be perhaps the most important persuasive tactic you have in your tool kit. Listening to your prospect will give you most of the information you need for a successful persuasive conversation. By listening and paying careful attention to the words and body language your prospect is communicating and by listening carefully for the words they don't say, you'll be able to discern most of what you need.

There is still, however, information beyond that. By listening with deliberate intent, you make the prospect feel respected and understood. In some cases, this feeling is the most important part of the transaction.

By listening actively, you'll be able to ask thoughtful and insightful questions. Asking better questions will give the impression that you're already invested in delivering quality. Not only will the impression you make be appropriate, but you will gather crucial information that could influence the success of your interaction.

When listening is your primary technique, your prospects will notice this consciously or subconsciously and they will want to listen to you, and reciprocate that attention.

Listening isn't just hearing words, it requires an overall comprehension of the story being told. In many cases, individuals are not as clear and concise at expressing themselves, as you've become. So listening to the conversation and finding the key components is up to you. Active listening also means paying attention to the sounds, tones, inflections, timbre, volume, and key used by the speaker. These details are also packed with information, revealing more insight about the speaker. By paying attention, you can determine someone's intentions, what they want you to think their intentions are, and what they expect of you.

If you have the opportunity, ask questions about the pieces that grabbed your curiosity, or that you're not clear about. This isn't just another opportunity to prove that you're a good listener, it's a prime time to ask questions that will draw out more information that you're seeking. This might mean asking your prospect questions that will cause them to express themselves in a certain way. You might be able to derive more insights from additional body language and other communicative behaviors. When you listen, acknowledge what's important to your prospect. See if you can determine the main argument and emotions.

THE FAVOR OF A SMILE

Your ability to smile is one of the most powerful tools to influence. This is true of influencing yourself or others. We've learned over thousands of years that the smile is a sign of happiness and friendship so the smile helps to lower our defenses. When individual smiles, dozens of influential processes happen automatically.

For yourself, when you smile, you're releasing neurotransmitters like dopamine, and serotonin into your body, which benefits in several ways. The body relaxes automatically when you smile. This relaxation reduces heart rate, blood pressure, general pain, and general stress. A smile is so powerful that it can strengthen one's immune system and increase one's endurance as endorphins are released.

For others, a smile from you to them communicates positivity and happiness. For them, this is a subconscious reminder of the happiness of other smiles they've experienced and releases good feelings, cultivating a generally happier mood and disposition. It doesn't take much; even a smile that lasts but a millisecond packs enough power to effect those who see it. Recent studies suggest even exposure within a sixteenth of a millisecond is still powerful enough to influence those who see it. The study exposed individuals to images of other people smiling, where exposure for 1/16th of a millisecond still influenced the group of individuals. Another set of individuals were exposed to images of people who were not smiling. At the end of the study, the participants were invited to all come to out to a venue for a complimentary night of music and free drinks. Those exposed to images of smiling people had more interactions, smiled more themselves, had more fun, and imbibed more drinks than those exposed to images of non-smiling people.

Remember that while speaking in anger can be used to rouse feelings of aggression, this is not the influence you're looking for. A forced influence is a short-lived influence.

THE POSITION OF VULNERABILITY

It used to be so, in business as well as other aspects of life, that showing any sign of vulnerability was not good. To show vulnerability was to show weakness, leaving yourself open to attack and exploitation.

Today, that's not so much the case anymore. To display vulnerability, to a client or anyone, is the starting point for innovation and change. A bit of vulnerability, real or implied, makes the impression that you aren't afraid to face the music and you're accountable for what you say and do.

One way to demonstrate personal vulnerability is to be yourself. Often, we hide a part of ourselves because we're worried about how it will be interpreted and what others will think. To be your true self puts you in a vulnerable spot. Others see this as bravery and they subconsciously want to follow your lead and be themselves, too. They may not do it, but they at least reminded that they want to live bravely and be their true self.

THE INFLUENCE OF EMPATHY AND FORGIVENESS

The ability to understand and related to another's feelings and experiences is yet another technique that can increase your powers of persuasion. If you want to use positive manipulation to drive an interaction, it helps to know who you're working with. We like people who are like us, so if a prospect is sharing information with you, be empathetic. Doing so generates a sense of inclusion for your prospect and that feeling of understanding and acceptance is your ticket to influencing an interaction.

Nod your head. Show concern. Show that you can relate to the stress or happiness of a situation in the same way the prospect has reacted. All of this helps you to be more relatable to the prospect which builds excellent rapport. The empathetic person has a much better chance of influencing a person or situation if relatability is already built into the rapport.

One of the key points to the empathetic approach is to capitalize on a perfect sense of timing. Sometimes a nod, a smile, an eyebrow raise, if done at the wrong time, can be distracting and off-putting for your prospect. Laughs and smiles, in particular, are important to get right. A misplaced laugh (or smile) amidst a devastating part of your prospect's story, is not going to build an empathetic rapport. It will build skepticism and distrust.

Practicing empathy means you'll have to put aside any feelings of superiority or pride. Where empathy puts you on the same playing field with your prospect, a sense of superiority will take you off again. You can't just try to cover up your sense of superiority; it's not about making sure the prospect doesn't see your attitude. If this is your frame of mind, you'll likely miss most of the details of communication.

Forgiveness is just as important an ingredient, necessary for some kinds of conversation and communication. If a history of bad feelings has existed between two people or groups for a long time, forgiveness is sometimes the only act that can initiate a successful and beneficial breakdown of those old feelings.

Forgiveness has roots in survival for our species. The act of forgiveness has, over thousands of years, helped to protect us. When we forgive someone, the benefit of that act is actually our own. It may feel nice to know for your subject that you forgive them and still accept them, but the relief you feel yourself when you forgive someone is tremendous. Letting go mentally and emotionally of the wrongs done to you is cleansing for you.

Forgiveness has also helped us, through the ages, to solidify an effective and efficient social structure within communities and groups. When an individual does something to go against a society's fundamental mores and customs, that individual is often subject to some version of shaming within the community. But forgiving the individual and letting them back into the group once the lesson has been learned is a very common way to practice unconditional love for group members. This practice can also strengthen one's loyalty to a group, for having been brought back into the group even after breaking fundamental social codes.

By practicing forgiveness you build healthier relationships and improve your mental health and state. Practicing forgiveness reduces the symptoms of depression and anxiety, and improves heart health in the form of lowered blood pressure and heart rate. Knowing that you're strong enough to forgive someone can also generate feelings of accomplishment, capability, confidence, and strength. Self-esteem improves. All of these changes to the mental and emotional state are evident in the interaction, making you a calm and collected individual with the confidence and power to forgive. Your demeanor will echo this.

THE STRENGTH OF SILENCE

In many interactions that will cross your path, the best response is no response. The simple practice of staying silent can offer huge influence over an interaction. It can be a tricky practice because we're naturally so uncomfortable with extended silence within an interaction. But what you'll find is that when strategically timed and placed, silence in an interaction can be a powerful leverage. The right silence can grab a listener's attention. The right silence can shakedown your prospect and get them nervous about not taking your offer. The right silence can convey appreciation, anger, astonishment, confusion or disapproval. Used at the right time and spot, the art of silence can convey many emotions and engage your prospect more, not less.

It's been said of debate and negotiation, that the individual to speak first is the one who loses. Holding your tongue to gather an ounce more information from your prospect gains you more leverage in the interaction. This is an early-taught tactic passed down from sales master to protégé. Business owners are privy to this tactic as well, as a defense against master sales vendors.

If someone makes you an offer, you can refuse. If it's the first offer, you should refuse.   The idea here is to communicate to your prospect that you don't need the deal as badly as they do and that you're not afraid to walk away.

You can test this silent manipulation (in an innocuous and playful way) with one of your friends to see if you can influence them. The next time a friend suggests you get together, try the following and see what they do next:

Friend: Let's meet up for a game this weekend.

You: A game, hmmm…. (silence)

Let your silence linger a bit longer than you normally would. Chances are your friend will be prompted to say something to justify the meetup.

Friend: Yes, we haven't gotten together in a while.

Your silence will be a subconscious cue to your friend that you seem to be considering whether or not it's worth it to meet up. So the next thing they say will be something to support or justify the idea of coming together. Not only will your friend be subconsciously aware that you might not find value in getting together for coffee, but your friend will also get a cue that you might not find them as valuable a friend. This will increase their nervousness of being rejected and they'll may be influenced by you to emphasize their worth. Obviously, this is an experiment you can test out which is short-lived and not harmful. Don't continue to repeat this over and over, however, or you may just lose your friends.

Similarly to silence, consider using the whisper technique. Place a whisper strategically into conversation to accentuate the call-to-action. By whispering to your audience or listener, you're creating a sense of secrecy and trust immediately. Not only is it an effective method for building rapport, but it sends a subliminal message about urgency and discretion.

CHAPTER 13: COVERT PERSUASION, TACTICS, AND TRICKS

This is the most persuasive form of covert persuasion. By *covert*, we mean that the tactics are crafty and unsealed, and people may never know or notice that you are using them; but in the end, the tactics will easily convince people to do what you want. Covert persuasion is aimed at creating change in clients' and customers' minds without them noticing. These changes convince them to purchase goods; an investor also endorses an idea that you have. To make the persuasion effective, one has to use correct words. For one to successfully use covert persuasion, it is advisable to follow eight easy steps.

1. Identify a targeted situation. This is something that is always stressing the targeted person. If you help the client identify the problem and solve it, such as high costs, you are helping them get a whole load off their back.

2. Help customers realize addressing their issues will help solve problems, like imposing high costs. Address the problem first before you start promoting your product on how much help it can offer the client.

3. Ask the clients to pinpoint a favorable outcome. It is difficult for clients to choose a better outcome. Questions that will mostly trigger them, like "What would you prefer best for this project?"

4. Ask customers to single out various consequences associated with the new outcome. This is very helpful, as it helps them prepare for the new outcome that will lead them to form a new idea that will make them consider your merchandise or service.

5. Have a confirmation that they want the new outcome. The clients sometimes may tell you something they think is what you want. As a good service provider, make sure that they are honest about what they

genuinely want, and this will make the process of persuading them easy.

6. Be certain that the new outcome is good for the clients. You have to acquire a good reputation by making sure that the customer benefits from your products and service and not only for short-term glory.

7. Always avoid being judgmental over a customer's negative responses. A client's point of view might vary from yours. You have to be patient by trying to understand their point, and maybe, in the end, you might see the point they are trying to put across.

8. Never at one time tell a client that they are wrong. They tend to be defensive and will try to prove that their point is right, and they might end up clinging to that point till the end.

In covert persuasion, twelve keywords are considered to be very persuasive. They are known to evoke feelings and get people's attention and interest. They include *you, results, health, discovery, easy, proven, safety, love, money, guarantee, new,* and finally, *save.* While answering the client, use compelling words, and you will find out that most people tend to agree with you more.

Covert persuasion works well when you predestine the desired outcome. One thing you have to note is that persuasion starts in the mind; the sooner you make your idea clear in your mind, the better it is since you will be able to know what you want. The thing that holds back people from being successful with their ideas is that they never focus on what they want exactly. This is contrary to successful people. Succeeding here requires discipline, effort, concentration, and the desire to not settle for less. Covert persuasion is also used to persuade people to move from saying no to saying yes. To be able to do this, you must know how people make their decisions. You have to change their fear of saying yes.

After persuading people successfully, they should be glad and never at any time regret taking the advice. But this is altered by a phenomenon called option of attachment. For example, a man has to choose between two ladies who have different personalities but are both good choices. After thinking for days, he comes to a decision and selects one of them. As soon as he makes his choice, one might think that he is very happy, but the fact is that now he sees the other lady better than days before. The man starts to think that the lady he dumped was much more attractive and that he has lost. This is precisely what happens when customers want to choose a product that two firms are offering. When he thinks for too long, he ends up feeling that choosing is losing. People tend to feel loss when they have to choose between two things.

To solve this phenomenon, never allow a client to develop a sense of attachment to two or more choices. This will ensure that the client will not end up feeling a sense of loss after choosing the other product. Secondly, ensure that if you must take the client through more than one product, then move quickly from a less attractive to a more attractive option. Never allow a customer to develop a sense of connection to a product that you know he will end up not getting. Discuss the less attractive options one by one as you tell the client why they need to be detached from the choices. Here you can use the experimental influence. This is done by giving the less attractive product to the client, allowing him to take it home and try working with it to see if it meets his standards. This will lower his option of attachment when he sees the product is not working to meet his expectations. At times, you can use the option of attachment to your advantage since it will be difficult for a customer to let go of your product and in the end, he/she will end up purchasing it.

CONCLUSION

Thank you for making it through to the end of NLP, let's hope it was informative and able to provide you with all of the tools you need to achieve your goals whatever they may be.

Anyone can learn how to work with NLP. It is not a secret that is just meant for some. The problem is that too many people are held back by not understanding what NLP is all about and they may decide that their morals don't allow for this kind of behavior. Because of this, they are going to shy away from even hearing about NLP, despite all of the benefits that this can bring to them.

This puts you at a distinct advantage over the others. And since most people aren't expecting this to occur to them, you are going to end up being the winner in the long run.

When you are ready to learn a little bit more about NLP, especially when it comes to dark NLP< make sure to use this guidebook to make sure that you get started on the right track.

Finally, if you found this book useful in any way, a review on Amazon is always appreciated!

www.ingramcontent.com/pod-product-compliance
Lightning Source LLC
Chambersburg PA
CBHW061800250726
48657CB00001B/207